RAF BOMBER COMMAND
and its aircraft 1941-1945

RAF BOMBER COMMAND
and its aircraft 1941-1945

James Goulding & Philip Moyes

LONDON

IAN ALLAN LTD

First published 1978
Reprinted 2002

ISBN 0 7110 0788 8

Published by Ian Allan Publishing

an imprint of Ian Allan Publishing Ltd, Hersham, Surrey KT12 4RG.
Printed by Ian Allan Printing Ltd, Hersham, Surrey KT12 4RG.

Code: 0204/A

Title page: Elegant lines of the Lanc are seen to advantage in this pleasing study
of N Squared (N²) of No 576 Squadron, a unit in No 1 Group.

Right: Fine aerial portrait of a Mosquito B.IV, the initial bomber mark used by
Bomber Command,

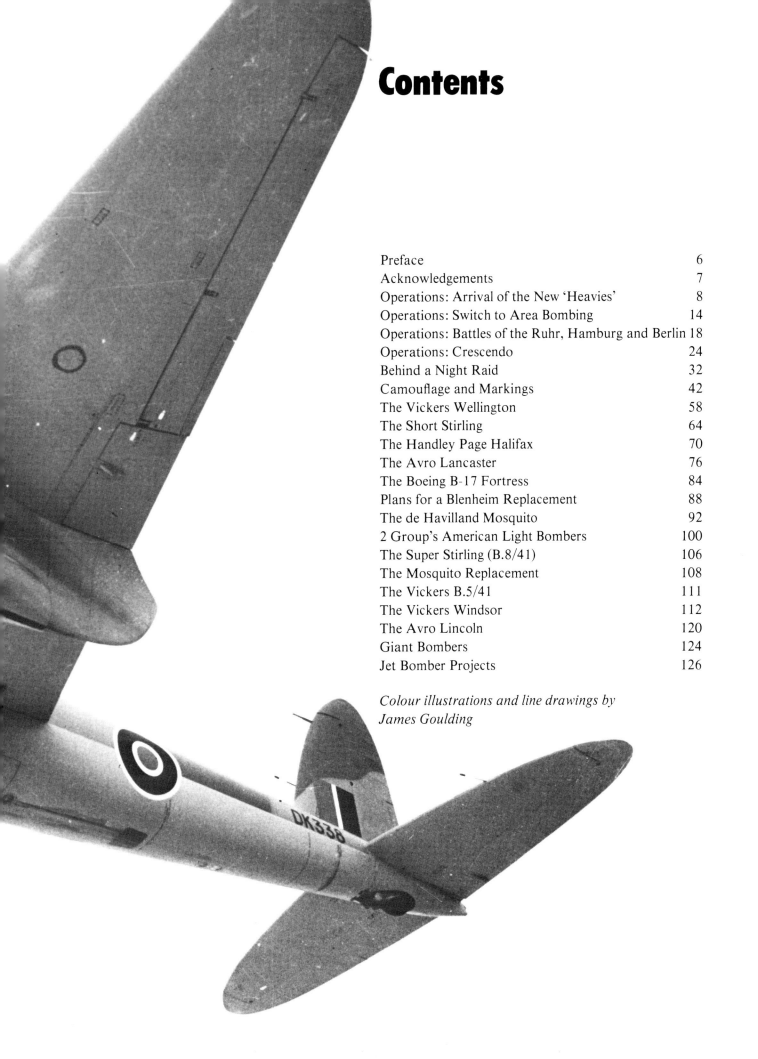

Contents

Colour illustrations and line drawings by James Goulding

Preface

The first volume of this work told the story of RAF Bomber Command from its formation in 1936 until the end of 1940, when the Command was still very much in its infancy, and struggling bravely to hit back at the enemy despite all manner of handicaps. This second, and concluding, volume tells the story of how the Command continued its tough, uphill battle and made a contribution to victory which the official *History of the Strategic Bombing Offensive* (HMSO, 1961) rightly sums up as 'decisive' — defined in the *Oxford Dictionary* as 'deciding, conclusive (especially decisive battle)'.

The continued development of such famous bombers as the Wellington, Lancaster and Mosquito is covered, together with that of all the other operational types. Also described are three prototypes flown during the war but not used in it — the

Buckingham, Lincoln, Windsor, and the various bombers of American origin which served with the Command. Notable among these were the Boston, Ventura, Mitchell and Fortress. The Liberator is also mentioned, but only briefly, for reasons stated elsewhere. Following the pattern of Volume I, a considerable portion of the text is devoted to the relatively little-known bomber aircraft projects of the period which never left the drawing board.

As before, the emphasis is on the bombers themselves, and with modellers as well as historians in mind, there is a special section devoted to contemporary camouflage and markings, including specially-prepared full colour artwork.

G.J.G. and P.J.R.M.

Acknowledgements
The authors wish to express their gratitude to the following helpers who so readily gave them their kind assistance during their search for information: E. B. Marsh, Hawker Siddeley Aviation, Kingston; E. B. Morgan, British Aircraft Corporation, Weybridge; J. D. Oughton, British Aircraft Corporation, Filton; and Brian Wexham, Vickers Ltd.

Wellington IIIs and Xs of 30 OTU, Hixon, Staffs. Special Night undersurfaces, fuselage sides and fins and rudders. Type C1 roundels and Dull Red code and aircraft letters and serials.

Operations: Arrival of the New 'Heavies'

As related in Volume I, Bomber Command was employed chiefly in the defensive role during the first year of war, although in the autumn of 1940 it had been able to resume its intended role of attacking German industry. Bitter experience in daylight raids during the early months of hostilities had forced the main force to concentrate on night operations, but this had brought problems of navigation and identification. No radar or navigational aids were yet available and thus crews often spent half an hour or more trying to find their specified target; they were seldom successful and the cumulative effect of their sorties was negligible. On the other hand, losses due to enemy action were light, for the German defences against night attack were only in a rudimentary stage.

The second year of war saw Bomber Command struggling to expand yet continually beset with difficulties and frustration. It remained organised on a basis of five operational groups, but in size and composition the force as a whole changed very slowly. Although the first really 'heavy' bombers were introduced in the winter of 1940/41 and the ensuing spring, technical problems repeatedly caused their withdrawal from operations. There were also serious delays in the production of these new types with the result that the Wellingtons and obsolescent Hampdens, Whitleys and Blenheims continued to fly the great majority of sorties throughout 1941. Indeed the Wellington, reliable but slow and inadequately armed, was to be the backbone of the main force until well into 1942.

First of the new heavies* to enter service was the Short Stirling which joined 7 Squadron at Leeming, Yorks, in late 1940 and eventually began operations from the 3 Group grass airfield at Oakington, Cambs, on the night of 10/11 February 1941, when three aircraft were sent to drop 56 x 500lb bombs on oil storage tanks at Rotterdam. Undercarriage collapses were one of the Stirling's teething troubles and belly landings were frequent — as was the need for the long-suffering ground crews' physical exertions to get the crippled bombers out of the mud!

Second of the new breed of bombers to enter service was the twin-engined Avro Manchester, which first reached 5 Group's 207 Squadron in late 1940 and operated for the first time on 24/25 February 1941. Target was a Hipper class cruiser at Brest and although all six Manchesters completed the mission, dropping a total of 70 x 500lb SAP (steel armour piercing) bombs in the target area, one crash-landed on return to base, due to an hydraulic failure

*At this time Hampdens, Wellingtons and Whitleys were classified as heavy bombers, and Battles and Blenheims as medium bombers. When the four-engined types entered service they became heavy, the Hampdens etc medium, and the Blenheims light. These rapid changes in terminology are confusing, even more so as the process has since continued and today all these aircraft would be correctly classified as 'light bombers'.

Right: Captain and crew of an early Halifax bomber of No 76 Squadron have a last minute chat underneath the wing of their aircraft before take-off from their base in Yorkshire in 1942.

and the incorrect assembly of the emergency air system preventing one of the undercarriage units from locking down. No results of the bombing were observed by the bomb aimers as the Manchester's transparent nose did not allow them adequate vision. This necessitated modification action to incorporate a new transparent panel.

The Manchester was continually jinxed by technical troubles, largely connected with its hitherto untried Vulture engines, and, although seven squadrons of 5 Group were eventually equipped with the type, its unserviceability was such that it was frequently

The Avro Manchester, seen in these three views, was a failure due largely to protracted teething troubles with its Rolls-Royce Vulture engines. It first entered service with No 207 Squadron in November 1940 and although it supplanted the Hampden in No 5 Group its career in first-line service was comparatively brief and by mid-1942 it was withdrawn in favour of the Lancaster, its four Merlin-engined derivative.

grounded for several weeks at a time. Indeed on one or two occasions squadrons had to revert temporarily to Hampdens. Crews developed a strong dislike for the Manchester, which was hardly surprising because during both operations and training sorties many accidents occurred, often with tragic results. Engine bearings seized, propellers feathered unaccountably, and tail flutter was encountered when climbing with full load. The latter was soon remedied, but, although several other difficulties were duly overcome, the basic problem of unreliable engines stubbornly remained. Under-powered and over-heating, they were unable to lift the Manchester above the critical flak level, and if one engine failed the bomber quickly lost height. It is no exaggeration to say that the Manchester was one of the RAF's biggest disappointments, yet had it not existed it is very probable that the highly successful Lancaster would not have been built.

The third new British heavy to become operational was the Handley Page Halifax. It began to reach 35 Squadron in 4 Group in late 1940 and first went into action on 11/12 March 1941, just five months after the completion of the first production aircraft. The primary target that night was Le Havre dockyard, and of the six Halifaxes despatched from Linton-on-Ouse, all but one bombed it. The sixth was unable to find the target, and having insufficient fuel for the journey to the alternate (Brest), was forced to jettison its bombs in the sea. Tragedy marred the mission, for one of the successful aircraft was mistaken on the return trip for an enemy raider and shot down in flames at Normandy, Surrey, by one of our own Beaufighters. Only two of the crew escaped by parachute and survived.

Hydraulic failures continually dogged the Halifax during its early weeks in service. When it became clear that hydraulic locks were not sufficient to ensure that the undercarriage remained retracted, particularly after damage, the hydraulic system was completely redesigned, much of the work being done at Linton-on-Ouse. Another source of trouble was the tailwheel. This retracted

forwards and was prone to remain retracted on landing, which often meant that most of 35 Squadron's ground personnel would have to crawl under the fuselage of a stricken 'Hallybag' and act as human jacks since the real things were not yet available. Not surprisingly, perhaps, the retractable tailwheels were soon abandoned.

At the beginning of 1941 Bomber Command's main objective remained the destruction of Germany's oil resources, but in March the Prime Minister, Winston Churchill, greatly concerned at our mounting shipping losses, issued a directive ordering top priority to be given to the Battle of the Atlantic for the next few months. Thus Bomber Command was diverted from its real task once again, and thereafter much of its effort, instead of being directed against oil and other industrial objectives, was switched to naval targets. Most notable amongst these were the battle-cruisers *Scharnhorst* and *Gneisenau* at Brest, the U-boat bases at Lorient and Bordeaux, and the great naval construction yards at Kiel in Germany itself.

By mid 1941 German U-boat and Focke-Wulf Fw200 attacks in the Atlantic had waned (albeit primarily due to naval countermeasures, rather than Bomber Command's efforts), and with the launching of the German attack on Russia a new directive was issued to Bomber Command by the Air Ministry which stated that the main effort was to be directed towards dislocating German transportation and civilian morale. It was considered that the concentration of air attacks on communication centres would prove of direct assistance to the Russians, and although the emphasis thus reverted to the strategic bombing of Germany, much effort still had to be directed against naval targets. On several occasions in 1941 small forces of Hampdens and Wellingtons and/or the new Stirlings and Halifaxes made daylight raids, sometimes with some degree of fighter protection. Targets included Kiel, La Pallice and Brest, and unlike the forays over Heligoland in 1939 the raids did achieve some success. For instance, against the fringe French target of La Pallice on 18 December 1941, at least five direct hits were scored

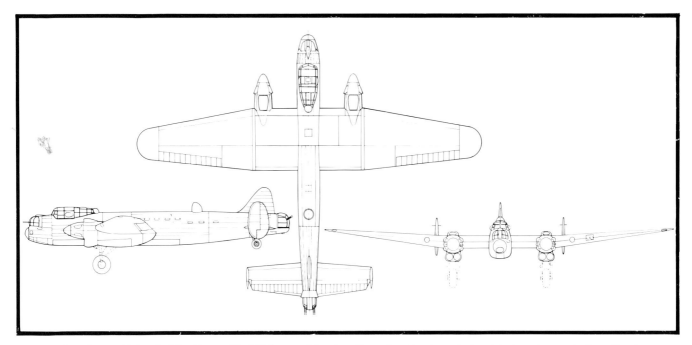

on the *Scharnhorst* which sailed for Brest with 3,000 tons of flood water inside her. Even so, the bomber casualty rate on this occasion proved severe. Fifteen Halifaxes had been put up, together with a fighter escort, and 14 of the bombers reached the target area, where they encountered between 12 and 18 Messerschmitt Bf109s and intense flak. Five Halifaxes were shot down and the rest were damaged.

Meanwhile the strategic night-bombing offensive was being waged whenever circumstances permitted, but due to the lack of

Above: Avro Manchester in the original squadron service form. Manchesters were eventually fitted with the twin-finned Lancaster tail unit.

Below: In to land comes a Blenheim IV of No 105 Squadron of No 2 Group. Note the gun position under the nose and the light external bomb carriers beneath the rear fuselage. / *IWM*

Above right: Rare flying shot of the second of two Hampden Mk IIs powered by Wright Cyclone engines. The type was never used operationally but this particular machine did see operational service with Bomber Command after conversion to Mk I standard.

navigational aids, it was achieving relatively little success. A survey based on crew reports and night photographs taken in June and July 1941 showed that, of those aircraft claiming to have hit their target, only about a third did in fact drop their bombs within five miles of the aiming point. Worse still, when the target was in the Ruhr, a region notorious for its industrial haze, the proportion was down to one in ten. The situation would have seemed hopeless had it not been for the fact that radar aids to navigation were at long last being evolved for Bomber Command.

Further hope for the future lay in the gradual introduction of bigger and better bombs. In March 1941 the first two 4,000lb high-capacity bombs, or 'cookies' as they were popularly known, were dropped on Emden by specially modified Wellington IIs of 9 and 149 Squadrons, with devastating results to civilian housing. Preceding this blast bomb, however, was a smaller version, the 2,000lb HC, which was in fact a modified sea mine and, like the latter (and also the so called 'land-mine' blast bombs of the Germans), had a tail parachute. This 2,000-pounder was carried by 5 Group's Hampdens, the aircraft still mainly used for sea-mining.

At the beginning of 1941 enemy night fighters were not common over Germany, but by the autumn, largely due to the Germans having established a large number of efficient ground control stations, they were encountered all too frequently and posed a serious threat. On 7/8 November, when 400 bombers were sent to Berlin, Mannheim, the Ruhr and elsewhere, 37 of them failed to return. Further losses of this magnitude could not be risked, and on 13 November Sir Richard Peirse was told the War Cabinet had decided that the command should conserve its strength in order to build up a strong force to be available by the following spring.

In the meantime, 2 Group, the light, tactical element of Bomber Command, had been seeing its share of action and suffering from similar frustrations to those of the main strategic force. During the early part of 1941 the group had sent small formations of its Blenheims to attack coastal or so called fringe targets in Germany and occupied Europe by both day and night, the day raids usually being made in cloudy weather, which offered the bombers some protection from the enemy's defences. Early in March, however, the emphasis in daylight operations switched to attacks on shipping in

the North Sea and English Channel, although raids were still made on fringe targets. Gradually, a series of fighter-escorted daylight raids known as 'Circus' operations was mounted against some of the fringe targets in the hope of bringing the Luftwaffe to battle. In addition to 2 Group's Blenheims, the heavier types, including occasionally Stirlings of 3 Group, were employed on these 'Circus' operations. However, the whole scheme proved disappointing because the escorting Spitfires lacked the range to cross the German frontiers and the bombing was thus confined to occupied territory about which the Germans cared less than their homeland. The Luftwaffe thus tended to intervene only when the tactical situation favoured it.

During their various daylight missions 2 Group's Blenheims usually flew at low level to achieve surprise, but this brought additional hazards. Aircraft were lost in collisions with ships' masts, and, in a particularly daring attack on the power stations at Cologne on 12 August, one Blenheim was seen to have its tail cut off by a high tension cable. Altogether, 12 of the 54 Blenheims taking part in the Cologne raid were lost, all but the aforementioned aircraft being shot down by flak over the target or by enemy fighters. This experimental deep penetration of Germany was not repeated.

A squadron of Boeing Fortress Is, 90 Squadron, was on 2 Group's strength during 1941 but its operational career was brief. 90 Squadron, contrary to American advice, was given the job of operating these early, inadequately equipped Fortresses, in the high-altitude day-bombing role, and from the beginning the scheme was a tragic failure. The squadron never had more than nine on strength at any given time and sent the Fortresses to attack singly or in twos and threes, beginning with a much publicised raid on Wilhelmshaven on 8 July 1941. It soon became painfully obvious that these totally misnamed Flying Fortresses could neither fly high nor fast enough to avoid German fighters, and lacking power-operated turrets or sufficient guns they could not defend themselves well enough. At the end of September 1941, following the loss of three Fortress Is in action and four more in accidents, the surviving aircraft were withdrawn from Bomber Command and either sent to the Middle East or transferred to Coastal Command.

Operations: Switch to Area Bombing

On 8 January 1942, Sir Richard Pierse left Bomber Command and his successor, who assumed command on 22 February, was Air Marshal A. T. Harris, a powerful and forthright personality who was to remain C-in-C until the end of the war. Harris had commanded 5 Group in 1939-40 and had later acted as Deputy Chief of Air Staff at the Air Ministry. Then, from mid-1941, he had been in charge of the RAF Delegation in Washington. He was convinced that strategic bombing could bring Germany to her knees, and it was his intention to do this, given a large enough bomber force, by reducing the great industrial towns to rubble. The Allied armies would be needed only to mop up after the devastating blows of the bombers. Harris was to remain true to this aim throughout the remainder of the war. Furthermore, he became an equally staunch supporter of area bombing, although, contrary to the oft-held impression, the decision to switch to this from selective attack was made before he arrived at Bomber Command. Attacks which would wipe out entire industrial cities and also have the effect of gradually breaking the morale of Germany's entire civil population had, in fact, been discussed by the policy-makers in 1941 when Harris was in America, and the decision to concentrate on an all out offensive of this nature was conveyed to Bomber Command in a new directive on 14 February 1942, just six days before Harris became C-in-C. The Command was instructed to strike with full force for the next six months at the industrial cities and towns of West and North-West Germany.

Once again, an attempt was to be made to break the morale of the civil population, and the industrial workers in particular. This time, however, the area bombing technique was to be employed; an aiming point would be chosen in the centre of each target city and a high proportion of incendiaries used to set the city well ablaze. High explosive bombs would also be dropped to crater roads, destroy electricity, gas and water mains, etc, and also prevent the progress of the fire-fighters.

At the outset, the force at Harris's disposal, excluding five Blenheim squadrons of 2 Group, mainly used as 'bait' in the Circus operations over France and for night intruder sorties against German night fighter airfields, amounted to 44 squadrons, of which 38 were actually operational. Only 14 of the 44 were equipped with Stirlings, Manchesters, Halifaxes and Lancasters, the remainder having the three old stagers of 1940, the Wellingtons, Whitleys and Hampdens. Harris thus began his long campaign with a total force of some 600 aircraft and a normally available force of only 300, including 50 heavy bombers.

The first German town that Harris's crews sent up in flames was Lübeck, one of the old Hanseatic ports on the Baltic, on the night of 28/29 March. Lübeck was one of several targets selected as alternatives to the principal industrial towns in the Ruhr, and soon after this raid Rostock, another Baltic port, suffered a similar fate. Four attacks were made on Rostock on four consecutive nights bringing the total acreage devastation in Germany up to 780, and, in regard to bombing, about squaring our account with Germany.

The general morale of Bomber Command at last rose markedly as a result of these two successes and encouraged Harris to stage a full-scale mass area attack on a major German industrial city by a

Sea mines are delivered by WAAFs to waiting Hampden bombers of No 408 'Goose' Squadron, RCAF. The parachutes which carried the mines gently down into the water can be seen folded in their tails.

force of approximately 1,000 bombers. This raid was eventually launched on 30/31 May, the target being Cologne, one of the four primary targets stipulated in the directive of 14 February 1942. For the raid Harris had not only to use the entire front line strength of Bomber Command, but also to borrow bombers from operational training units and other commands. The bulk of the force despatched comprised Wellingtons, Whitleys and Hampdens, 708 altogether, and with them went 338 of the new Stirlings, Manchesters, Halifaxes and Lancasters, the latter (two aircraft of 44 Squadron, 5 Group) having operated for the first time on 3/4 March 1942. No less than 367 aircraft of the total 1,046 main force came from the training groups, others coming from conversion flights in some of Bomber Command's new heavy bomber squadrons. The bomber stream was divided into three waves, and as it wound its way across the North Sea, 50 Blenheims of 2 Group and Army Co-operation Command, and 37 fighters of Fighter Command took off to 'intrude' over enemy airfields, harassing fighters. They maintained their diversion until the attack on Cologne had been completed.

The attack was opened by *Gee*-equipped Wellingtons and Stirlings of 1 and 3 Groups, carrying high proportions of incendiary bombs, and was concluded by the main attack starting one hour later by the Halifaxes of 4 Group and the Manchesters and Lancasters of 5 Group, the remainder of the force spreading its attacks throughout the intervening period. *Gee* was a device which relied on pulse signals received from three ground stations in England and enabled navigators to pinpoint their individual aircraft's position. The first of the new navigational aids to reach Bomber Command, *Gee* had initially been tried, experimentally, over enemy territory in August 1941 but had not entered service until the spring of 1942 when sets were available in sufficient quantity to make its use worthwhile.

Each bomber was strictly controlled on the Cologne raid and flew to the city in a predetermined position in the stream. The stream technique was being employed for the first time by Bomber Command, and one of its aims was to concentrate the attack in space and thus evade many of the night fighters individually patrolling certain sectors of sky. Its other aim was to concentrate the attack in time, thus saturating and, it was hoped, reducing the effectiveness of the enemy's ground defences.

Above: Preparing the sting. Bombs being finally adjusted before being loaded into the open bomb bay of a Mosquito B.IV of No 105 Squadron at Marham, Norfolk, in December 1942.

Below: Bostons of No 2 Group, including aircraft of No 88 Squadron coded RH, stand by to take part in the famous Dieppe Raid of 19 August 1942. / *British Official*

Below right: RAF Bostons over the target during the big daylight raid on the Philips radio and valve works at Eindhoven, Holland, on 6 December 1942. / *IWM*

At Cologne the entire attack was concentrated into about two and a half hours as against an average of seven hours for previous attacks, and 41 bombers failed to return, a loss rate of 3.8 per cent. Considering that the raid took place on a moonlit night and was the first time that some of the bomber crews had been into action, the results were highly satisfactory. Widespread damage was caused to Cologne; reconnaissance photographs taken on the morning after the raid revealed that 600 acres of the city, including some 300 acres in the centre, had been completely destroyed.

Despite the failure of two further 1,000 bomber attacks against Essen and Bremen, owing to cloud over the targets causing the bombing to be scattered, Bomber Command had now shown that it could, if given the tools, finish the job. Churchill gave the Command his wholehearted support and ensured that the production of heavy bombers and radar navigational aids, and the development of more efficient bombs and bomb sights were at last given top priority.

The rest of 1942 was spent in working out the new tactics, and the most important development, perhaps, was the formation of the Path Finder Force (PFF), soon to achieve group (No 8) status, on 15 August 1942.

The PFF was designed to take advantage of the new radar devices that were now becoming available. As these, or at least the later and better marks of them, were always in short supply, they had to be used by selected crews who marked the target with powerful pyrotechnic bombs, usually called markers or target indicators (TIs). The main force then used these TIs as aiming points. At the outset the PFF comprised five squadrons, one from each operational group of Bomber Command, but eventually it grew to 19 squadrons (by April 1945) equipped with Lancasters and Mosquitos. PFF crews were hand-picked from volunteers with at least 30 operational sorties to their credit.

In 1942, 19 new squadrons were formed in the command but, as Harris explained in his memoirs: 'Thirteen of these were taken from us. And of the new squadrons that were left to us, three were on more or less permanent loan to Coastal Command and engaged in anti-submarine patrols.'

Even so Bomber Command's striking power was very substantially increased by virtue of the fact that, whereas at the beginning of the year the bombers were mainly mediums, by the end of February 1943 the four-engined heavies made up two-thirds of the force, which meant that bomb carrying capacity increased by nearly seventy per cent. During this period the Whitleys, Hampdens and Manchesters were withdrawn and 2 Group's Blenheims were replaced by newer types — Bostons, Venturas, Mitchells and, most important of all, Mosquitos.

2 Group, which was always the smallest group in Bomber Command, continued to be mainly employed on daylight raids against fringe targets until May 1943, and from the Command's viewpoint it always seemed a misfit. Harris himself said that it 'had really nothing to do with our main striking force and the main offensive', and he was not sorry when it was transferred, with the exception of its two Mosquito squadrons, to Fighter Command on 1 June 1943, prior to becoming part of the newly formed 2nd Tactical Air Force.

Commonwealth and Allied squadrons had figured in Bomber Command's order of battle since 1940/41, and in January 1943 the handful of RCAF squadrons already in existence were banded togther into 6 (RCAF) Bomber Group, based almost entirely in Yorkshire. This unique group eventually grew to 14 heavy bomber squadrons flying Lancasters and Halifaxes, and its cost, with the single exception of the pay and allowances of attached RAF and other non-RCAF personnel, was borne by the Canadian Government.

Operations: Battles of the Ruhr, Hamburg and Berlin

By the beginning of 1943 Bomber Command not only had a sizeable force of heavies but was also introducing into service the two revolutionary blind bombing radar aids, *Oboe* and *H2S*. *Oboe* depended on signals transmitted from ground stations and enabled PFF Mosquitos to find and mark their target in all but the worst of weather. Although its short range restricted it to the Ruhr, the cities in that area which had hitherto enjoyed protection from industrial haze, searchlight glare, and an elaborate system of smoke-screens, decoy fires and lighting, could now be accurately marked for the main force. *H2S* was an airborne device which provided a rough radar map of the ground over which the bomber was flying. It was eventually carried by PFF Mosquitos and main force heavies. It was less accurate than *Oboe*, but on the other and it had no range restriction.

In January 1943 the British and American leaders sat in conference at Casablanca and, among other things, agreed a policy for the air bombardment of Germany, which was embodied in the so called 'Point-blank' Casablanca directive of February. This stated that both Bomber Command and the US 8th Air Force were to participate in 'the progressive destruction and dislocation of the German military, industrial and economic system; and the undermining of the morale of the German people to a point where their capacity for armed resistance is fatally weakened.' There followed a list of target systems and the intention was that the Americans would make precision attacks with their B-17s and B-24s by day, and Bomber Command area attacks by night — a joint round-the-clock offensive with a common objective: the utter destruction of German industrial power.

The directive naturally pointed to the Ruhr, and within that mighty arsenal, to Essen as the prime target for Bomber Command's area bombing offensive. On the night of 5/6 March 1943, Harris sent 442 bombers to Essen to deliver the opening blow of a sustained attack against Germany that was destined to last exactly a year. The target was accurately marked by four *Oboe* Mosquitos of 109 (PFF) Squadron whose red TIs were backed up with green ones dropped by some heavy bombers of the PFF. The bomb aimers of the main force only had to find these coloured markers and aim their bombs at them. An analysis of target photographs taken during the raid suggested that 153 crews had dropped their bombs within three miles of the Krupps works, and against such a difficult target as Essen this was an unprecedented success. Daylight photo reconnaissance confirmed that many acres of Essen were devastated and that the Krupps works themselves had received heavy damage.

This historic attack on Essen opened what became known as the Battle of the Ruhr, which raged until July and saw immense damage done, not only to towns such as Duisburg, Dusseldorf, Dortmund and Bochum in the Ruhr itself, but also to targets in

Right: Moonlight sonata. A Lancaster I runs up its four Merlin engines ready for take off during the Battle of Berlin in the winter of 1943/44. / *British Official*

places as widely separated as Berlin, Stettin, Pilsen, Munich, Stuttgart and Nuremburg, which were attacked during the same period. The campaign included 43 main attacks involving the despatch of 18,506 sorties, from which 827 aircraft failed to return, a casualty rate of about five per cent, not counting the many bombers which were damaged or destroyed in crashes after recrossing the English coast.

Harris was undaunted. The Battle of Hamburg was about to start and more new brainchildren of the 'back room boys' — the scientists — were available to help smash the enemy. Most spectacular of these was *Window*, metallised strips which, when dropped from the bombers during passage over enemy territory, gave the same indication on a radar screen as did an aircraft, thus flooding enemy control screens with multitudinous true and false responses. Other devices now available included *Boozer*, a receiver which lit a warning lamp when the aircraft became 'illuminated' by an enemy radar transmitter, whereupon the pilot would change course until the lamp went out; *Monica*, a rearward looking radar set designed to give warning of fighters approaching from astern; *Mandrel* for jamming the enemy's early-warning radar system; and *Tinsel*, which jammed German ground-to-air radio telephone frequencies.

So important did these and other radio and radar countermeasures become that in November 1943 a special group, No 100, was formed in Bomber Command for the sole purpose of using them to confound and destroy the enemy's night defences. It

eventually comprised 13 squadrons: 192 Squadron, using Wellingtons at first, then Halifaxes and Mosquitos, ranged over enemy territory to detect signals from new radar devices, a highly dangerous job when, as sometimes happened, the aircraft acted as live bait for prowling enemy night fighters. 199 Squadron (Stirlings then Halifaxes), 214 Squadron (Fortresses), and, later, 171 (Halifaxes), 223 (Liberators then Fortresses), and 462 (Halifaxes) Squadrons used various radio and radar jamming devices. Finally, seven squadrons of fighter Mosquitos hunted patrolling enemy night fighters, destroying on average three per night by the use of *Serrate IV* or *Perfectos*. Some of the Mosquitos also sought out German fighters on the ground during low level intruder raids against their bases.

The opening blow of the Battle of Hamburg was delivered on 24/25 July 1943, and it was on this occasion that *Window* was used for the first time. It scored an immediate and spectacular success, the tinfoil-backed paper strips utterly confusing the

Above: An 8,000lb block-buster bomb is prepared for loading into a Lancaster in late 1943. / *British Official*

Above right: Flares light the way — a view seen by many Bomber Command crews during the night offensive. / *RAAF Official*

Below right: Ready to go, Halifax B.V Series I (Special) bombers of No 76 Squadron await their turn to take off at their base at Holme-on-Spalding Moor, Yorkshire, in late 1943. / *British Official*

Bomber Command Order of Battle — 4 February 1943

Unit	Location	Aircraft	Strength	Unit	Location	Aircraft	Strength
1 Group	BAWTRY			*4 Group*	YORK		
12	Wickenby	Lancaster	21	10	Melbourne	Halifax	31
		Wellington II	1	51	Snaith	Halifax	25
101	Holme	Lancaster	18			Whitley V	2
		Wellington III	1	76	Linton-on-Ouse	Halifax	18
103	Elsham Wolds	Lancaster	19	77	Elvington	Halifax	19
		Halifax	1			Whitley V	1
460 (RAAF)	Breighton	Lancaster	17	78	Linton-on-Ouse	Halifax	18
		Wellington IV	1	102	Pocklington	Halifax	17
166	Kirmington	Wellington III	21	158	Rufforth	Halifax	27
199	Ingham	Wellington III	20			Wellington II	1
300 (Polish)	Hemswell	Wellington III	8	429 (RCAF)	East Moor	Wellington III	16
301 (Polish)	Hemswell	Wellington IV	12			Wellington X	2
305 (Polish)	Hemswell	Wellington IV	10	466 (RAAF)	Leconfield	Wellington X	16
100*	Grimsby	Lancaster	20	431 (RCAF)●	Burn	Wellington X	19

* Forming. Non-operational

● Non-operational

Unit	Location	Aircraft	Strength	Unit	Location	Aircraft	Strength
2 Group	HUNTINGDON			*5 Group*	GRANTHAM		
88	Oulton	Boston III	15	9	Waddington	Lancaster	19
107	Gt Massingham	Boston III	19	44	Waddington	Lancaster	16
226	Swanton Morley	Boston III	14	49	Fiskerton	Lancaster	16
105	Marham	Mosquito IV	18	50	Skellingthorpe	Lancaster	19
139	Marham	Mosquito IV	10	57	Scampton	Lancaster	17
		Blenheim V+	13	61	Syerston	Lancaster	19
21	Methwold	Ventura	16	97	Woodhall Spa	Lancaster	16
464 (RAAF)	Feltwell	Ventura	20	106	Syerston	Lancaster	17
487 (RNZAF)	Feltwell	Ventura	21	207	Langar	Lancaster	22
98	Foulsham	Mitchell	20	467 (RAAF)	Bottesford	Lancaster	24
180	Foulsham	Mitchell	19				

+ Used for training

Unit	Location	Aircraft	Strength	Unit	Location	Aircraft	Strength
3 Group	EXNING			*6 Group* RCAF	ALLERTON		
15	Bourn	Stirling	20	405‡	Beaulieu	Halifax	18
75 (NZ)	Newmarket	Stirling	15	408	Leeming	Halifax	15
90	Ridgewell	Stirling	15	419	Middleton St George	Halifax	16
149	Lakenheath	Stirling	17	420	Middleton St George	Wellington III	18
214	Chedburgh	Stirling	15	424	Topcliffe	Wellington III	19
218	Downham Market	Stirling	16	425	Dishforth	Wellington III	18
115	East Wretham	Wellington III	17	426	Dishforth	Wellington III	19
138 (Spec Duties)†	Tempsford	Halifax	15	428	Dalton	Wellington III	10
161 (Spec Duties)†	Tempsford	Lysander	8			Wellington X	5
		Halifax	5				
		Hudson	1	*8 Group (PFF)*	WYTON		
		Havoc	2	7■	Oakington	Stirling	21
		Albemarle/Hudson	2	35	Graveley	Halifax	23
192 (Spec Duties)†	Gransden Lodge	Halifax	2	83	Wyton	Lancaster	19
		Wellington X	12	109	Wyton	Mosquito	19
		Mosquito	3			Wellington IC	2
		Wellington IC	2	156(½)□	Warboys	Lancaster	17
						Wellington III	8

† These squadrons under control of Asst Chief of Air Staff (I) No 161 has det't at St Eval on loan to Coastal Command.

‡ Temporarily detached to Coastal Command
■ Lodger unit on 3Gp station
□ Re-equipping

enemy, who at one stage thought that 11,000 bombers were en route. The sky was cloudless and the Pathfinder crews, using their *H2S*, which gave the navigators a rough picture of the ground over which the bombers were flying, had no difficulty in marking the target for the main force.

Altogether, four massive RAF raids and two USAF daylight raids were made on Hamburg before the battle ended, and Hitler's propaganda minister, Dr Goebbels, described in his diary the damage done to the city as 'a catastrophe, the extent of which staggers the imagination.' He was absolutely right, for the general destruction was on a greater scale, and more sudden and complete, than ever before seen in a city of that size during any war. The alternative dropping of blockbusters, high explosives and incendiaries in each of the night attacks made fire fighting impossible; small fires quickly united into huge conflagrations and these, in turn, led to firestorms of typhoon-like intensity in the course of which trees of 3ft diameter were pulled out of the ground.

Further heavy raids were made on Mannheim, Nuremburg and other large industrial centres, and on the night of 17/18 August 571 aircraft made a very successful attack on the experimental station at Peenemünde on the Baltic coast, which was engaged in the development and production of V-weapons. Then, as the hours of darkness grew longer, Harris switched Bomber Command's main

Above: When Stirlings became obsolete as first-line bombers they were extensively relegated to supply dropping to the various resistance movements and also mine-laying. Here an aircraft of No 75 (New Zealand) Squadron of No 3 Group is loaded with mines early in 1944.

effort to the German capital, and on the night of 18/19 November the Battle of Berlin began.

This battle lasted until mid-March 1944 and comprised 16 major attacks involving the despatch of 9,111 sorties, 7,256 of which were flown by Lancasters, 1,643 by Halifaxes, 162 by Mosquitos and 50 by Stirlings.

The Germans had greatly improved their air and ground defences since the Battle of Hamburg, and as a result Bomber Command's losses now became heavy. Altogether, 492 bombers were reported missing, a casualty rate of about six per cent; 95 were destroyed in crashes after regaining the English coast and another 859 returned home damaged.

The results of the Battle of Berlin were altogether very disappointing, although, in fairness to Bomber Command, the weather during this campaign was probably worse than at any other time throughout the war. The ground could seldom be seen and the Pathfinders usually had to mark the target with 'sky-markers' above the cloud.

Operations: Crescendo

By now the Allied leaders were making preparations for the invasion of Europe and for the next six months Bomber Command came under command of the Supreme Allied Commander, General Eisenhower. Targets in France were bombed, especially the French railway network, to isolate Normandy and delay German reinforcements coming up. Bomber Command also struck at enemy airfields within tactical range of the assault area and, on the night preceding D-Day itself, hit the coastal batteries guarding the approaches to the selected beaches.

Next, to help the Allied armies in enlarging their bridgehead and advancing towards Paris, heavy attacks were made in daylight against enemy positions. It was decided not to waste time in training the crews to fly in formation like their USAAF comrades in arms, but to operate by day in concentrated streams, or gaggles as they were sometimes known, in the same way as by night.

Soon after D-Day, the Germans began to use their V-weapons. Bomber Command had been attacking and destroying their launching sites and storage depots ever since the beginning of the year. Four very large and elaborate installations, heavily protected by concrete, at Watten, Mimoyecques, Siracourt and Wizernes were completely destroyed. As a result of all this the scale of the V-weapon offensive was substantially reduced.

In September 1944 the bombers were formally released from their commitment to SHAEF and Harris was again able to use them for what he always considered to be their prime task, the strategic bombing of Germany. The Air Staff, however, had given oil targets priority and Harris did send the bombers against oil plants quite frequently. In conjunction with the USAAF's bombers they did, in fact, practically destroy Germany's oil resources in the short space of a few months. The Luftwaffe became so starved of fuel that valuable petrol was reserved for operational flights and flying training virtually ceased. The standard of German fighter defence subsequently fell. A diversion was made in November to dispose of the *Tirpitz* which was sunk in shallow water after three hits with 12,000lb Tallboy bombs dropped by specially modified Lancasters.

Bomber Command was now operating regularly in daylight, thanks to the Allies having gained air superiority, and in December operated in strength 19 times by day and on 23 occasions by night. German communications suffered very serious damage. The short *Official History* notes that:

'The general effect of attacks on the means of transport was to deprive the enemy of almost all power to move. Even his armies, which, naturally, had priority, were unable, except at the cost of enormous efforts, to shift from one position to another. His civilian population was for all intents and purposes immobile.'

The Germans, immobilised, desperately short of fuel, their air power smashed, were unable to stem the Allied advance.

On 23 March Bomber Command Lancasters struck two heavy

Right: Devastation at Bochum, an important German industrial town in the heart of the Ruhr, seen at the end of November 1944. / *British Official*

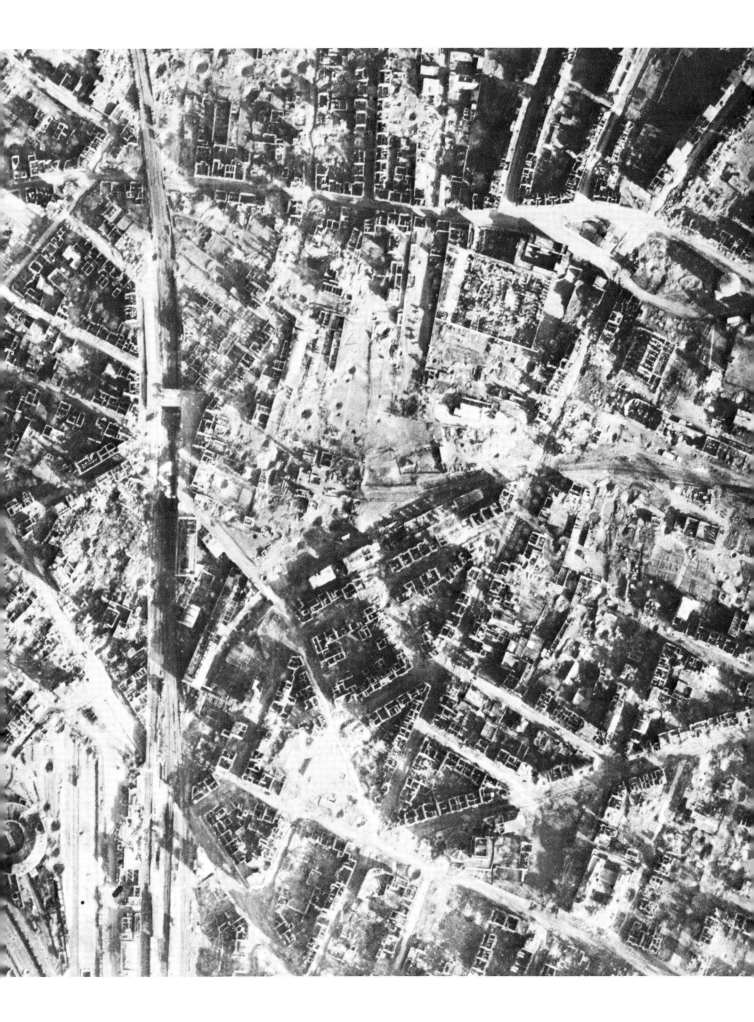

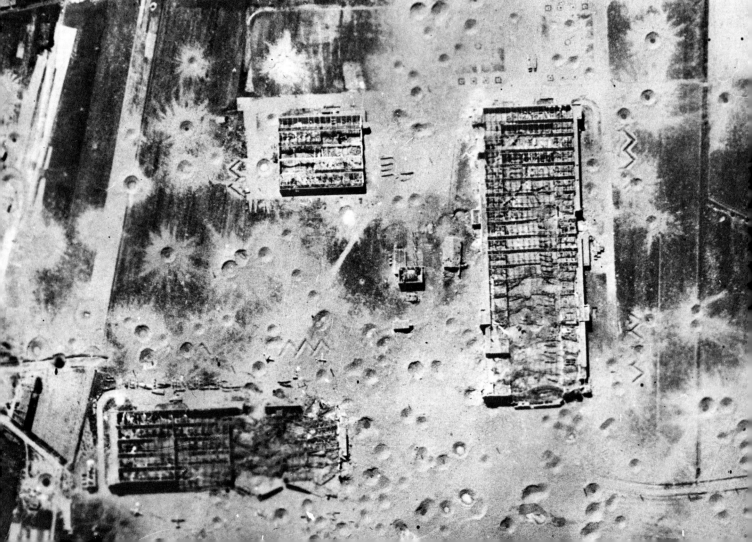

Above left: 'Our bombers were out in great strength'. Lancasters wing their way across a sunset sky after an attack on German targets in the Pas de Calais, Northern France, in the summer of 1944. / *British Official*

Below left: Severe damage to the three main buildings of the French SNCASE aircraft assembly plant at Toulouse after the attack by Bomber Command on the night of 1/2 May 1942. / *British Official*

Above: The capsised hull of the Tirpitz photographed in Tromso Fiord, Norway, more than four months after she was sunk by RAF Lancasters with 12,000lb Tallboy bombs. / *British Official*

blows at the little town of Wesel immediately before the crossing of the Rhine, north and south of the town, by Field Marshal Montgomery's 21st Army Group. Commandos captured the town that night with only 36 casualties and 'Monty' sent Bomber Command the following telegram:

'My grateful appreciation for the quite magnificent co-operation you have given us in the Battle of the Rhine. The bombing of Wesel was a masterpiece and was a decisive factor in our entry into the town before midnight.'

The end of the war was now very near.

Bomber Command's final wartime operations were on a humanitarian note. For bombs it substituted food and clothing and during the ten days between 29 April and 8 May 1945 it carried out Operation Manna, in which a total of 3,156 Lancasters and 145 Mosquitos dropped 6,685 tons of supplies to the starving Dutch in

Rotterdam, the Hague and other towns in Western Holland. Following the German collapse, Bomber Command flew back the bulk of our prisoners of war to this country, which enabled us to complete in a few weeks a task which, after World War I, took many weary months.

What part did the strategic bomber offensive play in the Allied victory?

It did not, as some people, including Harris, had hoped, bring about the complete collapse of Hitler's war machine without the need for an invasion, even with the tremendous help of the USAAF. In fairness to Harris, however, it must be recorded that although heavy bombers did at one time enjoy priority in production, the output achieved never rose sufficiently to enable the first-line strength of Bomber Command to exceed more than about 1,300 aircraft, not all of which were four-engined types. This was not enough to keep 1,000 bombers in action over Germany every 24 hours, the estimate Harris formed of the force he believed would be able to execute his plans.

The morale of the civilian population in German cities did not break, and in retrospect those who thought it would do so obviously overlooked the fact that Germany's population was firmly controlled by a ruthless police force. On the other hand, the bomber offensive forced the Germans to build up and maintain a strong home defence system of fighters, anti-aircraft guns, radar,

etc, which did create progressively more serious shortages at the other battle fronts. This system involved some two million men and women, including 900,000 anti-aircraft gunners, who might otherwise have performed more aggressive duties. Oil production in Germany was crippled and the Allied armies were saved many thousands of lives. Bomber Command alone assisted the Navy by sinking seven major warships, hampering U-boat production, and by the enormous mine-laying effort which sank several hundreds of ships and damaged many more.

Just under a million tons of bombs were dropped by Bomber Command; 625,000 tons fell on Germany and most of the remainder was dropped on targets connected with the war at sea. (For comparison, the total German bomb tonnage dropped on Britain, including the V-weapons, amounted to some 72,000 tons).

It should not be forgotten that for two whole years, Bomber Command, and Bomber Command alone, took the war not only to the enemy but to the very heart of his homeland. The results of these early raids proved to be disappointing, it is true, but it is equally true that the very fact that Bomber Command was hitting back at the enemy was a tremendous morale-booster to the British public, particularly those who had experienced the German 'blitz' on London, Coventry, Plymouth and elsewhere.

Throughout the war, Bomber Command demonstrated a remarkable versatility, tackling with success all sorts of sidelines, such as the sinking of warships, sea-mining, dam-busting, breaching sea walls, tactical bombing in support of the army, supply-dropping, operations in aid of Resistance movements in enemy-occupied territory, and many other interesting and important activities. Altogether, 392,137 operational sorties were flown by the Command on all types of operations, and the official history of the strategic bombing campaign sums up the combined RAF/USAAF effort by saying:

'Both cumulatively in largely indirect ways and eventually in a more immediate and direct manner, strategic bombing and also in other roles, strategic bombers made a contribution to victory that was decisive. Those who claim that the Bomber Command contribution was less than this are factually in error.'

Left: One of the Lancaster B.I (Special) aircraft which were specially modified to carry 22,000lb Grand Slam deep penetration bombs pictured during the raid with these weapons on the Arbergen railway bridge over the River Weser on 21 March 1945. / *British Official*

Below: A black-painted Liberator B.IV used for radio countermeasures by No 223 Squadron of No 100 Group in the closing months of the war. / *via Alfred Price*

Bomber Command Order of Battle — 22 March 1945

Unit	Location	Aircraft	Strength	Unit	Location	Aircraft	Strength
1 Group	BAWTRY			*5 Group*	SWINDERBY		
12	Wickenby	Lancaster I, III	20	9	Bardney	Lancaster I, III	22
100	Grimsby	Lancaster I, III	19	44 (Rhod.)	Spilsby	Lancaster I, III	16
101	Ludford Magna	Lancaster I, III	32	49	Fulbeck	Lancaster I, III	19
103	Elsham Wolds	Lancaster I, III	19	50	Skellingthorpe	Lancaster I, III	17
150	Hemswell	Lancaster I, III	16	57	East Kirkby	Lancaster I, III	16
153	Scampton	Lancaster I, III	21	61	Skellingthorpe	Lancaster I, III	19
166	Kirmington	Lancaster I, III	27	106	Metheringham	Lancaster I, III	16
170	Hemswell	Lancaster I, III	18	189	Fulbeck	Lancaster I, III	17
300 (Polish)	Faldingworth	Lancaster I, III	20	207	Spilsby	Lancaster I, III	21
460 (RAAF)	Binbrook	Lancaster I, III	27	227	Balderton	Lancaster I, III	18
550	N Killingholme	Lancaster I, III	27	463 (RAAF)	Waddington	Lancaster I, III	21
576	Fiskerton	Lancaster I, III	19	467 (RAAF)	Waddington	Lancaster I, III	19
625	Kelstern	Lancaster I, III	29	619	Strubby	Lancaster I, III	17
626	Wickenby	Lancaster I, III	21	630	East Kirkby	Lancaster I, III	21
				617*	Woodhall Spa	Lancaster I, III	41
						Mosquito VI	1
3 Group	EXNING			83 (PFF)†	Coningsby	Lancaster I, III	22
15	Mildenhall	Lancaster I, III	22	97 (PFF)†	Coningsby	Lancaster I, III	19
75	Mepal	Lancaster I, III	26	627 (PFF)†	Woodhall Spa	Mosquito IV, XX, 25	29‡
90	Tuddenham	Lancaster I, III	21				
115	Witchford	Lancaster I, III	32				
138*	Tuddenham	Lancaster I, III	20				
149	Methwold	Lancaster I, III	30				
186†	Stradishall	Lancaster I, III	31				
195	Wratting Common	Lancaster I, III	30				
218	Chedburgh	Lancaster I, III	29				
514	Waterbeach	Lancaster I, III	32				
622	Mildenhall	Lancaster I, III	22				

* Special tasks
† On loan from 8 Group
‡ Includes 4 Mk IX, XVI

* Non-operational
† Only two of its three flights operational

Unit	Location	Aircraft	Strength
6 Group	ALLERTON		
RCAF)			
415	East Moor	Halifax III	18
		Halifax VII	6
420	Tholthorpe	Halifax III	24
425	Tholthorpe	Halifax III	22
408	Linton-on-Ouse	Halifax VII	24
426	Linton-on-Ouse	Halifax VII	25
432	East Moor	Halifax VII	24
424	Skipton-on-Swale	Lancaster I, III	20
427	Leeming	Lancaster I, III	20
		Halifax III	8
429*	Leeming	Lancaster I, III	19
		Halifax III	5
433	Skipton-on-Swale	Lancaster I, III	20
		Halifax III	1
419	Middleton St George	Lancaster X	23
428	Middleton St George	Lancaster X	25
431	Croft	Lancaster X	20
434	Croft	Lancaster X	19
		Lancaster I, III	5

* Non-operational

Unit	Location	Aircraft	Strength
4 Group	YORK		
10	Melbourne	Halifax III	25
51	Snaith	Halifax III	31
76*	Holme	Halifax VI	11
		III	29
78	Breighton	Halifax III	29
158	Lissett	Halifax III	29
346 (FAF)*	Elvington	Halifax VI	8
		Halifax III	18
347 (FAF)†	Elvington	Halifax III	18
		Halifax VI	5
466 (RAAF)	Driffield	Halifax III	19
640*	Leconfield	Halifax VI	10
		Halifax III	15
77	Full Sutton	Halifax VI	28
		Halifax III	19
102	Pocklington	Halifax VI	19
		Halifax III	1

* Operational Halifax III
† To re-equip Halifax VI 30.3.45

Unit	Location	Aircraft	Strength
8 Group (PFF)	HUNTINGDON		
7	Oakington	Lancaster I, III	19
35	Graveley	Lancaster I, III	19
83*		Lancaster I, III	
97*		Lancaster I, III	
156	Upwood	Lancaster I, III	19
405 (RCAF)	Gransden Lodge	Lancaster I, III	18
582	Little Staughton	Lancaster I, III	21
635	Downham Market	Lancaster I, III	19
105	Bourn	Mosquito IX, XVI	34
109	Little Staughton	Mosquito IX, XVI	36
128	Wyton	Mosquito XVI	24†
139	Upwood	Mosquito IX, XVI	14‡
		Mosquito XX, 25	14
142	Gransden Lodge	Mosquito 25	19
162	Bourn	Mosquito XX, 25	18
163	Wyton	Mosquito 25	17
571	Oakington	Mosquito XVI	29
578**	Graveley	Mosquito XX, 25	2●
		Mosquito XVI	9
608	Downham Market	Mosquito XX, 25	20
627*		Mosquito IV, XX	
692	Graveley	Mosquito XVI	25

* Detached to 5 Gp (qv)
† Incl. 1 Mk 25
‡ Operating Mosq. XX, 25
** Non-operational
● Re-equipping

Unit	Location	Aircraft	Strength
100 Group	BYLAUGH HALL		
23 (BS)	Little Snoring	Mosquito VI	28
85 (BS)	Swannington	Mosquito 30	18*
141 (BS)	West Raynham	Mosquito 30	11
		Mosquito VI	6
157 (BS)	Swannington	Mosquito XIX	10**
		Mosquito 30	12
169 (BS)	Great Massingham	Mosquito XIX	15
		Mosquito VI	4
239 (BS)	West Raynham	Mosquito 30	19†
515 (BS)	Little Snoring	Mosquito VI	23
171 (BS)	North Creake	Halifax III	19
192 (BS)	Foulsham	Halifax III	15
		Mosquito XVI	8
		Anson	—
		Mosquito IV	6
199 (BS)	North Creake	Halifax III	17
		Stirling III	2
462 (RAAF) (BS)	Foulsham	Halifax III	20
214 (BS)	Oulton	Fortress III	18
223 (BS)	Oulton	Liberator	14
BSDU	Swanton Morley	Mosquito VI	6
		Mosquito XIX	2
		Mosquito 30	3
		Mosquito II	1

* Incl. 1 Mk VI
** Incl. 2 Mk VI
† Incl. 1 Mk VI

Behind a Night Raid –
a look at how a bombing attack was planned and organised

'There were so many bombers over the target that my chief worry was in trying to avoid a collision.'

Thus remarked an RAF bomber pilot who took part in a heavy attack on Bochum, an important Ruhr target, on the night of 12/13 June 1943. There were in fact 503 bombers taking part in this raid but they did not collide. Instead, they dropped their 4,000-pounders, other HEs, and their incendiaries, circled round to see the result of their bombing, and came back home. And in the large majority of cases they no doubt arrived back at their bases at exactly the right time at which they were scheduled to return.

In the early days of the war when Bomber Command was still feeling its way, raid planning was relatively minimal and far from being an exact science. By the time the offensive began in earnest, however, things had changed considerably and the need for every raid to be planned thoroughly and with timetable accuracy became of paramount importance. Without timetable accuracy, saturation technique, which Bomber Command developed under 'Bomber' Harris's leadership, would not have been possible.

The bombers had to take off at the right time, arrive at their target at the right time, and return at the right time — not easy for those responsible for the organisation, but nevertheless achieved in a variety of operations. For the anniversary of Hitler's accession to power, Goering had arranged to make a speech to the Wehrmacht from the German Air Ministry in Berlin. It was going to be quite a grand occasion. The Germans had announced details of the 'dignified ceremony', as they called it, a few days beforehand. They had even told the public at what time radio sets should be tuned in, and at what precise moment Goering would speak. Eleven o'clock on the morning of 30 January 1943 was the great moment when the Field Marshal would start. But RAF Bomber Command was aware of the event and came to take a hand in the proceedings. At 11 o'clock precisely, three Mosquito B.IVs of 105 Squadron from Marham in Norfolk arrived over the German capital and dropped their bombs. Goering was sent ducking for shelter and his speech was postponed until noon. It was a perfect example of thorough planning and perfect timing. In spite of all the problems, distance, weather, enemy defences and so on, the Mosquitos arrived at precisely the right moment.

Marham-based Mosquitos provided a further instance of pinpoint timing when two formations, one each from 105 and 139 Squadrons, bombed Jena on 27 May 1943, an attack which rounded off their campaign of low-level operations which had begun a year earlier. It was essential for success that the Mosquitos should deliver their attack on the Zeiss optical works and the factories of Schott and Genossen, makers of raw and finished optical glass, just before dark. No sooner, no later. They had to have sufficient light to pick out their targets, and then the darkness for protection on the long flight home. The round trip covered a

Right: Lancaster take-off. Note the canopy of searchlights to mark the airfield, the line of the lamps marking the flarepath, and the light shone along the ground to help the aircraft. / *IWM*

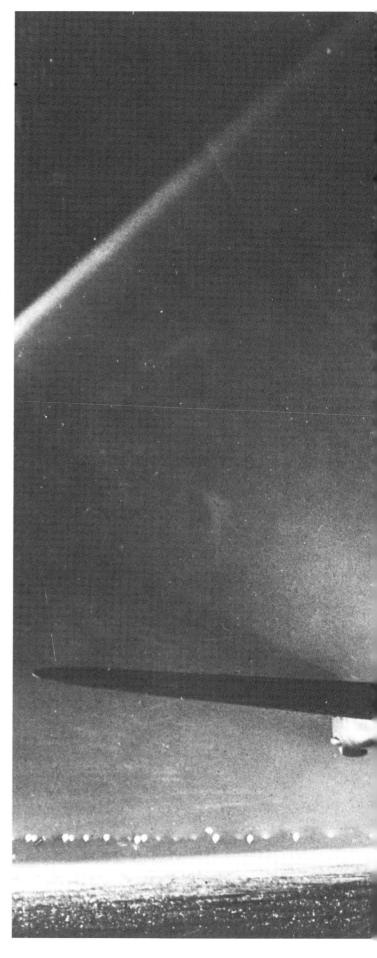

distance of well over 1,000 miles and, regardless of the route, some 500 miles of it had to be over German territory. Despite the consequent hazards, the Mosquitos arrived over Jena at their scheduled time, and arrived home at their scheduled time, having attacked a vital target in the heart of the Reich.

An earlier blow at Germany's U-boats conceived on similar lines was struck on 17 April 1942 by Lancasters of 44 and 97 Squadrons, from Waddington and Woodhall Spa respectively. They bombed the *Maschinenfabrik Augsburg-Nurnberg* plant at Augsburg which manufactured half the diesel engines used by the German submarine fleet, as well as other important war material.

Another notable daylight raid was made on 17 October 1942 when a large force of 5 Group's Lancasters bombed the great French armament factory at Le Creusot, about 170 miles southeast of Paris. The attack took place at about six o'clock in the evening, just as dusk was falling, and the Lancaster crews were instructed to complete their bombing in the shortest possible time. But they were not to bomb in formation; thus, this concerted attack called for perfect timekeeping on the part of each crew. The whole raid was successfully completed in about 20 minutes. In Bomber Command's heavy night raids the timing and organisation was on a wider scale. Defences had to be saturated by the speed and weight of the blows.

Let's see how a raid was planned and executed. But first a few words about the nerve centre where such plans were laid — Bomber Command headquarters. When the Command formed in 1936 it had a temporary headquarters at Uxbridge in Middlesex, but as these were considered too vulnerable to enemy air attack, efforts were made to find a more suitable site. At this stage a wing commander, Alan Oakeshott, DFC, suggested the area around his home at Walters Ash in the Chiltern Hills, just outside High Wycombe. Photographs of the area proved him to be right and by March 1940 the site at Naphill was ready for occupation. Wg Cdr Oakeshott died on operations over the Baltic in 1942 and his name is honoured on the nearby Naphill Memorial.

From the air the RAF station gave little away. Even from the ground there was little to show that it was not the country village and farmhouse it appeared to be, but the centre from which all Bomber Command operations were controlled. Nerve centre of the Naphill complex was the operations room, deep beneath a grass-covered tree-shaded mound, covered with bluebells in the spring, which concealed its concrete shell. Air-conditioned, floored with rubber, and indirectly lit, it was entered by a single door and had an extraordinarily tranquil atmosphere. Three walls of the lofty, oblong room were covered with maps, and on the main wall, opposite the single entry door which was reached by a stairway, there were three blackboards each about 30ft by 10ft. These displayed the Order of Battle. The C-in-C had only to glance at them to see at once the exact strength of every group, the whereabouts of the squadrons in it, and the total number of aircraft and crews available.

Every possible target was listed at Bomber Command in a secret file. This file, which was daily kept up to date, contained maps, photographs, plans, information on output, and notes on defences and the best way to evade them.

The general policy for the bomber offensive was formulated by the Chiefs of Staff on the basis of the reports and recommendations submitted to them. It was then approved by the War Cabinet, and their decisions were communicated through the Air Ministry in directives to the C-in-C, Bomber Command, whose duty it was to implement them and, in consultation with his operational staff, to

Right: Aircrew at a Royal Australian Air Force Halifax bomber base leave in transport for their aircraft, prior to taking off for a raid on Berlin. / *RAAF*

plan the actual bombing operations. Each day the C-in-C would hold a conference in the ops room at Naphill attended by the Deputy C-in-C (who was responsible for detail planning), the Senior Air Staff Officer (who set the operational machinery in motion), a naval staff officer, the Chief Intelligence Officer, the Senior Meteorological Officer, the ops room staff and liaison officers, including those from the US forces. The routine was as follows: At 0900 the C-in-C would appear in the ops room and the Senior Met Officer would forecast the weather for the coming night over our bases and everywhere in range. The Intelligence Officer than advised the C-in-C what objectives there were in the areas suitable for attack and with the aid of his priorities list he was then able to select targets in each category (eg oil, transport, industrial installations for the night's operations. Next, the number of aircraft and type of bomb load required were determined with the aid of tables compiled by the Operational Research Section, bearing in mind the details of the construction of the target, etc, supplied by the Chief Intelligence Officer.

It now fell to the C-in-C to choose H-Hour (time over target),

this being dependent on the weather over bases and target, tactics, the effort forseen for the following day, distance from bases and the amount of darkness available, and the necessity to link up with all the night's operations to produce the maximum confusion among the defences. 'Other ops' (eg mining) having been settled, the C-in-C left the conference and preliminary warning orders were passed to the groups concerned.

Detailed planning was now begun by the ops staff. Routes were worked out, the appropriate portion of the time over the target allocated to each individual group, aiming points selected and protection of the force arranged (with the aid of aircraft carrying radio and radar countermeasures). These details were then written down on a Form 'A' (Operational Order) which was passed to the ops room controller who put in a 'broadcast' telephone call to the controllers at all the groups and read out to them the 'order of batting' for the night. This was heard simultaneously by all the controllers who could interject or ask for information immediately. These orders were confirmed by signal.

Stage two of the proceedings was centred on each ops room of the groups where the controller consulted with his AOC, and air vice marshal, and the SASO of the group. They decided which squadrons should operate to fulfil the group's part in the operation, if necessary in consultation with the station commanders. The controller at each group then put in a 'broadcast' telephone call to their opposite numbers at the stations within their group and gave details of what each station had to do. They gave the target, the

Left: Crew members of a Lancaster don their Mae Wests and parachute harness in preparation for ops. / *IWM*

Below: Bomber Command's operations room located underground at High Wycombe. Directly facing the camera in centre background are Air Marshal Sir Richard Peirse, AOC-in-C from October 1940 to January 1942 and, on his left, AVM R. H. M. S. Saundby, the SASO. / *IWM*

time each squadron was to be over the target, and all other necessary details.

By about noon stage three was reached when these orders would have reached the ops rooms at each of the stations, where the controller would consult the station commander and squadron commanders about the aircraft and crews that had to take part. Crews were selected and lists of the pilots' names with time of briefing were posted in all messes and flight rooms. The squadron armament officers and maintenance officers, as well as the station intelligence officers, were given the details of the night's operation and the intelligence officer began to organise all the material necessary to enable the crews to be adequately briefed. The controller would arrange for the carefully timed departure of each aircraft and the corresponding time for the aircraft to bomb the target. Meanwhile, the navigation officers would work on the routes allocated by command HQ.

Elsewhere on the station there was equally intense activity as pilots consulted with aero-engine mechanics, gunners checked their guns and polished their turrets' Perspex, and every other crew member, both air and ground, busied himself with his appointed task. Eventually came the time for each aircraft to undergo its NFT (night flying test), a last minute check in the air to ensure that all was in order.

After checking that everything was satisfactory, the crews snatched some sleep as they did not yet know what the op was or how long the mission would take. While the crews slept, tractors would pull caterpillar-like trolleys of already fused bombs from the bomb dump to the dispersal points and the armourers would get on with the intricate task of bombing-up. Huge bowsers would give each bomber its quota of petrol, and from other sources the aircraft would receive their oil, oxygen, ammunition, cameras, etc.

As briefing time approached, in mid-afternoon, the detailed and standby crews would gather in the briefing room. They sat in rows, some smoking, some ready to take notes, while the station commander, or perhaps a squadron commander, announced the target for the night, which was pin-pointed on a large wall map behind him. After the inevitable 'ohs and ahs' had subsided the speaker would outline the reason for attacking the target in question and then deal with general tactics, making special reference to the operating height, the timing points, the length of time over the target and the exact details of the aiming point. The latest enlarged photographs of the target were thrown on to a screen by means of an epidiascope, and simplified maps of the objective, with flak, barrage balloon and searchlight dispositions marked on them, were issued to the navigators. The met officer, 'Cloudy Joe' in the bomber crews' parlance, would then take over and he would tell the crews what sort of weather conditions might be expected, including cloud formations and other important details. 'Cloudy Joe' was followed by the intelligence officer who gave all available information on enemy defences, including the location of flak batteries and night fighter airfields along the route, together with the suspected strength at each point. Next came the signals officer, who addressed the wireless operators in particular, informing them of the frequencies to be used for identification, fixes (positional signalling), homing and distress signals. The armament

Below: Early wartime scene in an operations room at a bomber station where the ops ordered by Command were worked out in detail. / *IWM*

Above right: Armourers belt-up .303in ammunition for the bombers' guns. / *IWM*

Below right: A 4,000lb 'Cookie' blast bomb is loaded into a Lancaster at a snow-covered airfield in East Anglia for an attack on Germany. / *British Official*

officer's advice, concerning the bombs, their nature and fusing, concluded the briefing. All was now set and the attack, always subject to the meteorologists' continued approval, was on.

Incidentally, briefing could last as long as three quarters of an hour or even more, although it was often shorter, and likewise the degree of formality. There was always an air of tension at first, although as the crews began to ask questions, which they were always encouraged to do, and work out the details of their mission the tension usually relaxed and the atmosphere became not unlike that of a university lecture room.

Briefing over, the crews were dismissed until their operational supper with its highly prized egg — a real one instead of the usual powdered variety — after which they either managed to get a little more rest or else straightaway donned their flying clothes. Sweaters, scarves, battledress, Mae Wests, and parachute harness; over the silk socks, the woollen stockings, and over these the flying boots lined with lambs' wool; then the flying helmet, with its oxygen mask. At the last moment they would snatch up their parachutes and bag of rations, containing biscuits, a few sweets and some fruit, and the thermos flasks of hot tea or coffee. The navigator also had his special bag of tricks.

The crew tenders, driven by WAAFs, would then pick them up and run them out to their aircraft, which loomed through the twilight like motionless pterodactyls. They would climb aboard, make the last minute checks, and then, one by one, the bombers' engines would burst into life; the heavily-laden aircraft, picked out by their navigation lights, would then begin to move, ponderously, in procession to the take-off point. The first one would turn slowly on to the head of the runway, pause to clear its engines, and then, with a roar of propellers in fine pitch, start to roll. As the speed increased it would bump once or twice and finally, as the runway lights raced past on either side, it would become airborne. No sooner were the wheels retracted and the bomber clear of the runway then those next in line took off in rapid succession. Presently all were gone.

The journey to the target had begun.

A selection of some of the bombs used by RAF Bomber Command in World War II, ranging from a 500lb medium capacity bomb to a 22,000lb Grand Slam medium capacity deep-penetration bomb. / *IWM*

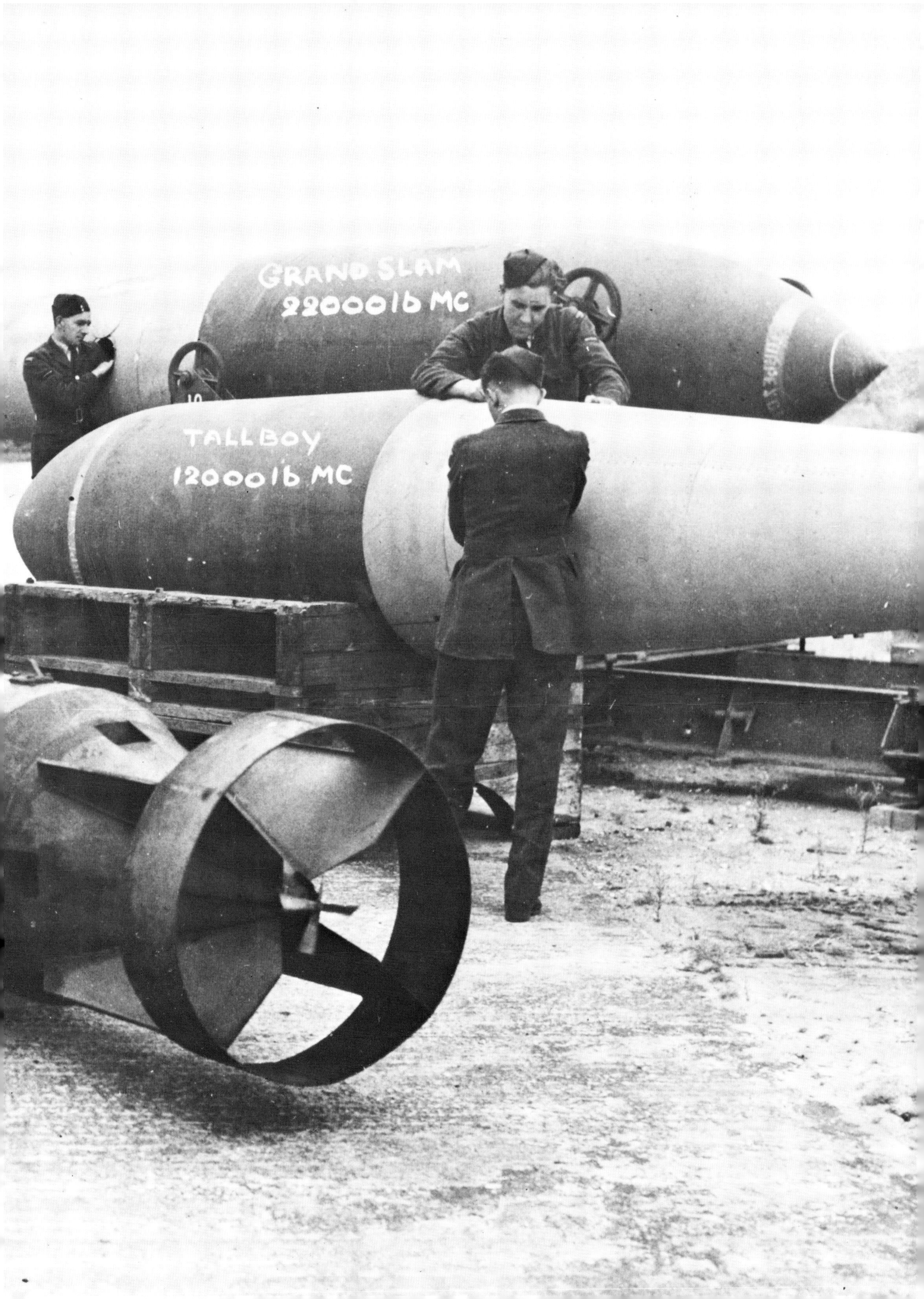
GRAND SLAM
22000 lb MC
TALLBOY
12000 lb MC

Camouflage and Markings

Wellington II W5379 in production camouflage scheme. Wavy top line to Special Night unofficial and later ordered to be straight. Serial number probably in white pending official directive ordering these to be painted Dull Red. / *IWM*

General schemes and markings

The winter of 1940/41 saw a wide variety of styles of camouflage and markings adorning the night bombers of Bomber Command, yet all conforming to the contemporary official specifications. At the beginning of 1941 the official scheme for night flying bombers consisted of an upper surface pattern of Dark Earth and Dark Green, with all under surfaces painted in Special Night, RDM2A. The Special Night finish was to be extended up the fuselage sides for three quarters of the width. The upper wing roundels were to be Type B and the fuselage side roundels were to be Type A1. Underwing roundels were not to be carried. The aircraft serial number was to be painted in Dull Red on the Special Night finish immediately forward of the tailplane.

The squadron code and individual aircraft letters were to be painted in Medium Sea Grey. A fin flash was to be carried. Within these directives many individual interpretations were to be found, particularly with regard to the style of fuselage roundel and fin flash, to the positioning of code and aircraft letters and their size, and to the style of spraying the top boundary line of the Special Night areas on the fuselage sides. Some of the variations in the national markings were a legacy from earlier changes in official policy, and could be seen in the variety of roundel and fin flash sizes and styles. At each period of a particular markings standard, hundreds of aircraft flowed from the production lines and either went to squadrons or into store.

There were many occasions when, say, the fuselage roundel size was changed on an individual aircraft type for some reason — the Vickers Wellington, for instance, being a good example of this,

exhibiting a number of different sized Type A1 roundels during its production life. There still lingered in service, too, aircraft with fuselage roundels converted from Type A to Type A1. During the early part of 1940 Type A fuselage roundels were standard on all production bombers, in some cases of large diameter, and these were all converted by the addition of a yellow outer ring. At one period the Type A roundel used on the Wellington was very large and conversion of this roundel was often made with a narrow banded yellow ring. Some of these non-standard roundels continued in use into 1941. Some Wellingtons were delivered from the production lines with exceptionally large Type A1 roundels in spite of the tendency amongst squadrons to make fuselage roundels less conspicuous.

By far the most common fuselage roundel in use during the whole of 1941 and the early months of 1942 was the Type A1 of 49in diameter, a roundel in use on such types as the Wellington,

Below: A Handley Page Halifax B.I of 10 Squadron. This machine typifies the Halifax in the initial camouflage scheme, as delivered from the factory, with Medium Sea Grey code letters and aircraft letters added by the squadron. / *IWM*

Above right: Avro Manchester I L7284 of 207 Squadron, typifying the Manchester in its initial production markings, 1940/41. Medium Sea Grey squadron codes, aircraft letters and serial. Dark Green/Dark Earth/Special Night finish. / *IWM*

Below right: Halifax I of 76 Squadron in the typical night bomber camouflage scheme of late 1940 to mid-1942. The white rings and stripes of the national markings have been over-washed to lessen their brightness. The wavy top line to the fuselage Special Night areas was unauthorised. / *IWM*

Whitley, Halifax, Stirling and Manchester night bombers. The Hampden fuselage roundels, due to the thin, boom-like rear fuselage, showed much less variation and were generally Type A1 of 35in diameter. Some Blenheim day bombers delivered with Type A fuselage roundels of 35in diameter had a narrow yellow ring added to conform to the requirement. The Blenheim, as on other types exhibited a variety of roundel sizes, but the most commonly used Type A1 roundel on the Bristol bomber was of 45.5in diameter. Later in its production life the 35in fuselage roundel became standard.

Type B upper wing roundels showed less variation on individual types. On the Whitley, Wellington, Hampden and Blenheim, bombers long established in service and in production, the size of upper wing roundels had been decided during the early months of the war and there was little reason for any change in size. Standard Type B roundel sizes for these aircraft were as follows: Whitley — 84in; Wellington — 63in; Hampden and Blenheim — 66.5in. The Halifax and Manchester had 84in Type B roundels and the Stirling 77in.

Fin flash sizes continued to vary after 1941, as many bombers painted with long fin stripes during mid-1940 continued in service without having them converted to the new standard size of fin flash, which consisted of three 8in wide bands of Dull Red, White and Dull Blue, 27in high. This standard marking had been brought into use on the orders of the Air Ministry issued on 1 August 1940, but the painting of the new fin flash on individual aircraft was carried out when convenient, usually when the aircraft was taken out of service for repair or overhaul.

During 1941 there was considerable disquiet among bomber crews about the conspicuousness of fuselage roundels and fin flashes. These continued misgivings about the markings, which had first been voiced during 1940, had prompted squadrons to dull down the yellow and white areas of national markings. The 'top brass' of Bomber Command gave the problem considerable thought and evolved their own form of fuselage roundel to lessen the glare of the existing Type A1 roundel. The brightness of the Type A1 was proved during tests when a Wellington was flown over observers stationed at various points and illuminated by searchlights. Although the Wellington was flying at 20,000ft, its fuselage roundels could clearly be seen from the ground, appearing as a bright spot. Bomber Command favoured the adoption of a revised roundel similar in dimensions to a Type A, but with the white ring replaced by pale blue (possibly MAP Sky Blue) and a thin outer ring of yellow. It is not known if this roundel was ever used on operational aircraft, but it is thought unlikely because of the development by the Royal Aircraft Establishment at Farnborough of the Type C and C1 roundel. The RAE were asked to investigate the roundel problem and offer a solution. Their answer was the development of a roundel which had been scientifically calculated to have rings of equal reflectivity. Thus the

Above left: Bristol Blenheim IV R3816 of 107 Squadron. Dark Green/Dark Earth/Night finish. Medium Sea Grey code and aircraft letters. National markings overwashed with Medium Sea Grey on white areas. / *IWM*

Below: Vickers Wellington ICs of 311 Squadron. On these aircraft the fuselage roundels have had the white rings overpainted with Special Night to lessen their brightness in searchlight glare. / *IWM*

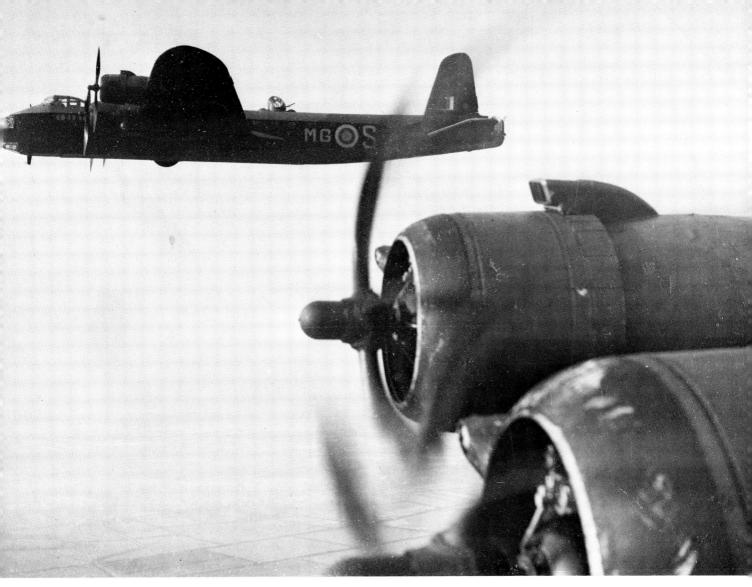

Above left: Wellington II W5461 of 104 Squadron. Medium Sea Grey code and aircraft letters. Dull Red serials. Fuselage roundels and fin flash washed over with Medium Sea Grey.

Below left: Whitley V Z9226 of 10 Squadron painted overall in Special Night. White rings and stripes of national markings painted out in Medium Sea Grey, which latter was also the colour of the code and aircraft letters. Dull Red serials on fuselage.

Above : Short Stirling I of 7 Squadron. National markings darkened. Small squadron code letters and large aircraft letter in Medium Sea Grey.

yellow and white rings were considerably narrower than the Dull Red and Dull Blue rings. Each ring reflected the same amount of light, producing a roundel of even tone when seen at any distance, without glare. The fin flash too was calculated to have similar effect, using a narrow white stripe.

Before the new national markings were officially adopted several months passed during which extensive tests were carried out, but in the meantime individual squadrons continued the process of reducing the glare of national markings. This usually took the form of entirely over-washing the markings with thinned darker paint, often Medium Sea Grey. At least one squadron, No 311, overpainted the white areas of the national markings with Special Night. This squadron's Wellingtons had very large Type A1 roundels at the time and there would have been little point in completely painting out the white areas and yet leaving the very large yellow outer rings, even though the deep yellow used was much less bright than the white areas. It is therefore possible that the yellow rings on these aircraft may have been overpainted in

Medium Sea Grey, as had been done on a night fighter squadron, No 85, which was also trying to make markings less conspicuous in searchlight glare.

Squadron code and individual aircraft letters continued to be painted in Medium Sea Grey for the most part, although there may have been a few cases where Sky Grey was used, but this was contrary to the general tendency to dull down light areas of markings. Certainly, photographs exist which show very light toned code and aircraft letters, and Sky Grey was an extremely pale grey — much lighter than Medium Sea Grey. Unfortunately, a print made on 'hard' paper can produce extremes of contrast from a negative, and could result in almost white letters on a dark ground tone, so that it is difficult to assess which grey was being used. Some wartime publications also quote code and aircraft letters as being painted in pale blue at this time, but the evidence for this is unknown. Bad mixing of large tins of Medium Sea Grey may have resulted in a more blue-toned version of that grey being used on some aircraft. Lighting conditions can affect the appearance of colours: Medium Sea Grey code and aircraft letters certainly had much more sheen than the surrounding Special Night areas, and this reflecting a blue, sunny sky would probably appear as pale blue to an observer, yet could appear as a medium grey on a dull, sunless day. So many wartime publications relied on personal observations of colours when describing camouflage schemes because official information and documentation was not easy to obtain. Interpretation of a colour used on an aircraft could be difficult and misleading if the observer was not familiar with the range of Ministry of Aircraft Production standard shades, and did not have samples of these for comparison. An observer might have a preconceived idea of a colour, and think, for instance, that Medium Sea Grey was a very pale grey (a popular misconception even today). On seeing the true shade, much darker than his idea of the colour, he could well report the colour in use as Dark Sea Grey.

Certainly, some wartime publications quote colour schemes that could not have come from official sources. Unfortunately, colour scheme information and colour samples were not freely available to everyone at that time, although all the colour schemes and changes were available, and acted upon, in aircraft factories. These were available in *Air Publication* 970, which was kept in every drawing office in order to comply with official directives on all aspects of design and construction of aircraft, including external and internal painting. This was continually amended by policy or technical changes, in lines as far as colour schemes were concerned, with the signals and telegrams sent by the Air Ministry to operational squadrons. As well as to the squadrons, markings changes were sent to the Resident Technical Officer (the Air Ministry representative resident at each company), who was responsible for seeing that these revisions were made as soon as possible to production aircraft. The camouflage and markings drawing would be continually amended on the instructions of the RTO as each change was authorised. Thus there was always a close affinity between squadron marking standards and those of aircraft companies. The Air Ministry sent a signal or telegram to the squadrons and RTOs. The companies amended their drawings and copies would be sent to squadrons. The only variation between factory and squadron in complying with a change of marking depended on individual interpretation. It was possible for two interpretations to appear in the same squadron — the squadron's own idea of the markings change and the officially-approved revision of the markings' drawing, which could be received by the squadron later. This was particularly true of the earlier war years, but later on there was much greater standardisation of markings and less variation.

The under surfaces of bombers became standardised during 1940 as Special Night (RDM2A) finish for night flying aircraft and overall Sky on day bombers, with roundels in use on the latter. This continued to be the normal finish for Bomber Command aircraft throughout 1941 and most of 1942. Night bombers continued to

Above: The original Merlin-Wellington prototype, L4250, modified to test the 40mm gun turret. Dark Green and Dark Earth upper surface finish with yellow undersurfaces.

Below left: Armstrong Whitworth Whitley V Z9302 in the ultimate 1940 colour scheme, with straight line to fuselage Special Night areas. This colour scheme was used until May 1942.

have the Special Night area extended up the fuselage sides, with a straight top line officially authorised, but in some cases interpreted as a rather irregular, and sometimes very wavy, line. The haphazard extension of the Special Night up the fuselage sides applied more to Service painting: new factory painted aircraft usually had the Special Night paint terminating in a straight top line, and as more and more of these aircraft entered service, the variations seen became less common.

In 1941 and 1942, 4 Group's Whitley squadrons adopted a non-authorised, but officially accepted, new finish of overall Special Night. This was used to achieve an overall matt finish without sheen, rather than for the camouflage effect, in the mistaken belief that Special Night was effective in delaying searchlight pick up.

In mid-May 1942 two important changes were made to bomber aircraft colour schemes: the Type C and C1 roundels and new less-conspicuous fin flash were officially adopted and ordered to replace the existing markings on all RAF aircraft. This was of special importance to bomber crews who were concerned about the problems of searchlight pick up. Another important change for the same reason was the order to replace the Medium Sea Grey code and aircraft letters with Dull Red ones. These two changes applied to both night and day bombers, and although primarily introduced to improve night camouflage the new markings were useful in reducing conspicuousness even in daylight.

On bomber aircraft the new roundels were standardised in two sizes: 36in diameter for small and medium-sized aircraft and 54in diameter for large aircraft. The new standard fin flash was also to be used in two sizes: 24in × 24in, or 24in high and 36in wide. In each case the white bar was 2in wide.

The revised night bomber camouflage scheme introduced in mid-May 1942 involving the change of roundel style to Type C and C1, change of fin flash to its new, revised form, and change of code and aircraft letters to Dull Red, remained in use for the rest of the war, except for one important revision — the abandonment of RDM2A Special Night paint. RDM2A paint had always posed problems in its use, despite the promise shown by the paint in early trials. In order to get a really matt, velvety finish, RDM2 was only just stable, and would rub off as a sooty mark on any object that

came in contact with it. Because of this it was difficult to get it to adhere to an undercoat. Ordinary Night paint proved to be the most successful, but it was always peeling away in the airflow. It was also found, from tests on a Mosquito fighter, that RDM2 created excessive drag due to its very rough surface finish, and this at a time when losses of Bomber Command aircraft were giving grave concern and when every effort was being made to increase heavy bomber speeds. The demise of RDM2 finally came about when it was discovered that ordinary Night black was much more effective than Special Night in evading searchlight pick up — the very reason for the development of Special Night in the first place. A very similar paint was developed in Germany for the painting of night bomber undersides, and it would be interesting to know if similar problems were encountered by the Luftwaffe on operations.

On 19 October 1942 the Directorate of Operational Requirements ruled that ordinary Night was to replace Special Night on all night flying aircraft, reverting, in fact, to the original bomber underside paint. This ruling left the RAF with 40,000gal of Special Night and 20,000gal of thinners surplus to requirements and totally useless.

Above left: Avro Lancaster I R5689 of 50 Squadron in the typical night bomber finish used from May 1942 to the end of the war: Dark Green/Dark Earth/Night. Dull Red code and aircraft letters, Dull Red serial.

Below left: Mosquito IV DZ313. Dark Green/Ocean Grey/Medium Sea Grey finish. Spinners are Ocean Grey.

Below: Wellington VI DR484 in high altitude finish. Dark Green/Dark Earth/Deep Sky. Yellow outer ring of fuselage roundel shows as black because of orthographic film. Deep Sky also appears lighter than true tone.

The roughness of the Special Night finish and the realisation that it was reducing the performance of heavy bombers led to another refinement to increase speed. Fighter speeds during the early days of the Battle of Britain were increased by the use of the Type S finish system, which included the use of smoother, more refined and less drag inducing paints. New paints manufactured to the new refinement standards, but retaining the same colours, were given the suffix Type S: thus Dark Green Type S, Dark Earth Type S and Sky Type S became the standard top coat paints on fighters. Eventually bombers, too, were able to take advantage of the benefits of the new paints, and thus the DOR notice of 19 October 1942 also ordered the change to Dark Green Type S and Dark Earth Type S for the heavies.

Therefore by the beginning of 1943 the camouflage of Bomber Command day and night bombers had evolved into standard finishes that were to remain in use for the rest of the war, the exception being Mosquito bombers which used a separate scheme, to be described later, together with other special colour schemes for aircraft undertaking specialised duties. Both day and night bombers had upper surface camouflage of Dark Green and Dark Earth in a disruptive pattern. Day bombers had the under surfaces painted overall in Sky, without roundels, and night bombers had an overall under surface finish of Night, again without roundels. The Night finish was extended up the fuselage sides for three-quarters of the depth, and was painted overall on each side of the fin or fins. The upper surfaces of the wings were marked with Type B roundels of varying size to suit individual aircraft types. The fuselage roundels were Type C1 of the sizes already quoted, and fins were adorned with the new fin flash. Squadron code and individual aircraft letters

were painted in Dull Red on both day and night bombers. Serial numbers were painted in Dull Red on night bombers and Night on day bombers, to contrast against the ground colours. The positioning of code and aircraft letters varied considerably: with the exception of the Lancaster, the positioning of code letters either in front of or rearwards of the fuselage roundel depended on the aircraft type and individual squadron. On Lancasters the fuselage roundels were positioned during production painting so as to give room for the squadron code letters to be placed forward of the roundel on the port side and aft of the roundel on the starboard side. Thus the roundel was closer to the wing trailing edge on the starboard side of the fuselage and farther aft on the port side, but in spite of this there were a few cases where this convenient spacing was ignored and the code letters were placed aft of the roundels on each side. In general, however, code letter positioning on the Lancaster was much less subject to variation than on other types. This system of painting the fuselage roundels was started on the Manchester and carried through on to the Lincoln. The first production Lancasters had fuselage roundels of 49in diameter in Type A1 style, with the standard 24in x 27in fin flash. Squadron code and aircraft letters were painted in Medium Sea Grey. After mid-May 1942 the fuselage roundel was changed to Type C1 of 54in diameter, with the fin flash changed to 24in high and 36in wide with a 2in white stripe. As on other types fuselage letters changed to Dull Red.

Mosquito bombers, because of their special characteristics of high speed and lack of defensive armament, were painted in a different manner to other day-bombers. The very first production PRU/bomber conversion Mosquitos were painted in the standard day bomber colours of Dark Green/Dark Earth/Sky, but this was soon replaced in service and on production lines by a new camouflage resembling that used by day fighters. This was to hide the true nature of the new bomber by giving the impression that it was a twin-engined fighter, and the colours were satisfactory for high-altitude daylight operations, although early in its career it was often flown on low-level strikes. The standard camouflage scheme for day-flying Mosquitos was an upper surface finish of Dark Green and Ocean Grey, with overall Medium Sea Grey on the under surfaces. Some of the earlier production aircraft, especially those converted from the Dark Green/Dark Earth scheme, may have been painted in Dark Green and the mixed substitute grey (7 parts of Medium Sea Grey and 1 part of Night) instead of the true MAP shade of Ocean Grey. To heighten the illusion of the aircraft being a day fighter some early Mosquito bombers, including examples from Australian and Canadian production lines, had Sky-painted spinners and an 18in rear fuselage band. Squadron code and aircraft letters were usually painted in Sky, but in the later war years they were often painted in Dull Red. Some night-operating Mosquitos, including the special *Oboe*-equipped marker aircraft, were painted overall in Night on their under surfaces. These aircraft had the Night areas extended up the fuselage sides to three-quarters of the width, and carried Dull Red serials on the dark areas. Mosquito bombers had Type B upper wing roundels of 54in

Above left: Halifax III PN167 of 347 'Tunisie' Squadron, Free French Air Force. Dark Green/Dark Earth/Night. Squadron codes in Dull Red outlined in yellow. Red diamond on fin. Blue used in national markings was lighter than the RAF Dull Blue. /*IWM*

Left: Mosquito B.XVI MM183 of 692 Squadron, No 8 (PFF) Group. Dark Green/Ocean Grey/Medium Sea Grey. Dull Red code and aircraft letters. Black serials. /*IWM*

Above: Wellington III of 425 'Alouette' Squadron, RCAF. Note Special Night areas on fin stripping off, a common fault with this black finish.

1
Size growth in Bomber Command: to the same scale, a Short Stirling I of No 15 Squadron is compared with a Handley Page Hampden I of No 44 Squadron.

2
A. W. Whitley Mk V of No 78 Squadron in overall Special Night finish. De-icing paint on leading edges; darkened areas in national markings.

3
Wellington Mk IC of No 301 (Polish) Squadron showing very large fuselage roundels.

4
Wellington Mk IC of No 311 (Czechoslovak) Squadron; white area of fuselage roundel painted out with Special Night.

5
Wellington Mk VI in high-altitude finish of Dark Green and Dark Earth on upper surfaces and Deep Sky on under surfaces.

6
Wellington Mk II of No 104 Squadron; national markings darkened to lessen brightness in searchlight glare.

7
Avro Manchester I of No 49 Squadron based at Scampton, Lincs, during 1942.

8
Handley Page Halifax B.Mk II Series I of No 35 Squadron based at Linton-on-Ouse, Yorks, midsummer 1942.

9
Handley Page Halifax B.Mk III of No 77 Squadron based at Full Sutton, Yorks, during 1944.

10
Avro Lancaster B.Mk I of No 149 Squadron based at Methwold, Norfolk, during 1944.

11
Avro Lancaster B.Mk II of No 115 Squadron based at East Wretham, Norfolk, early 1943.

12
de Havilland Mosquito B.Mk IV of No 105 Squadron based at Marham, Norfolk, December 1942.

13
de Havilland Mosquito B. Mk XVI of No 692 Squadron based at Graveley, Hunts, November 1944.

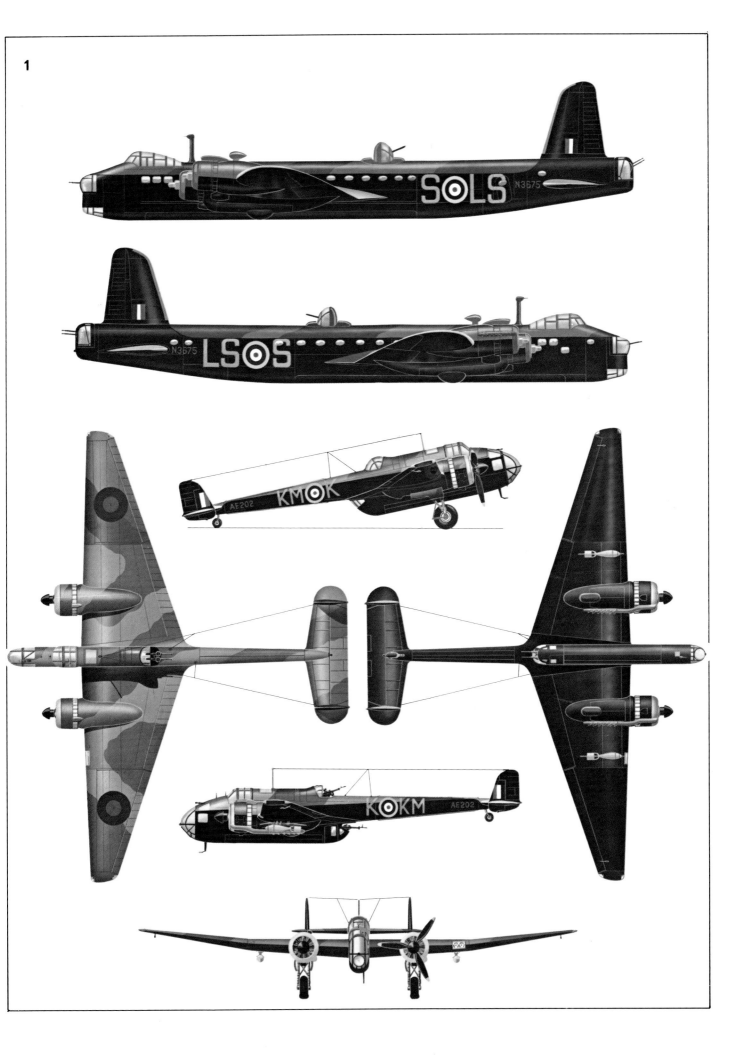

1

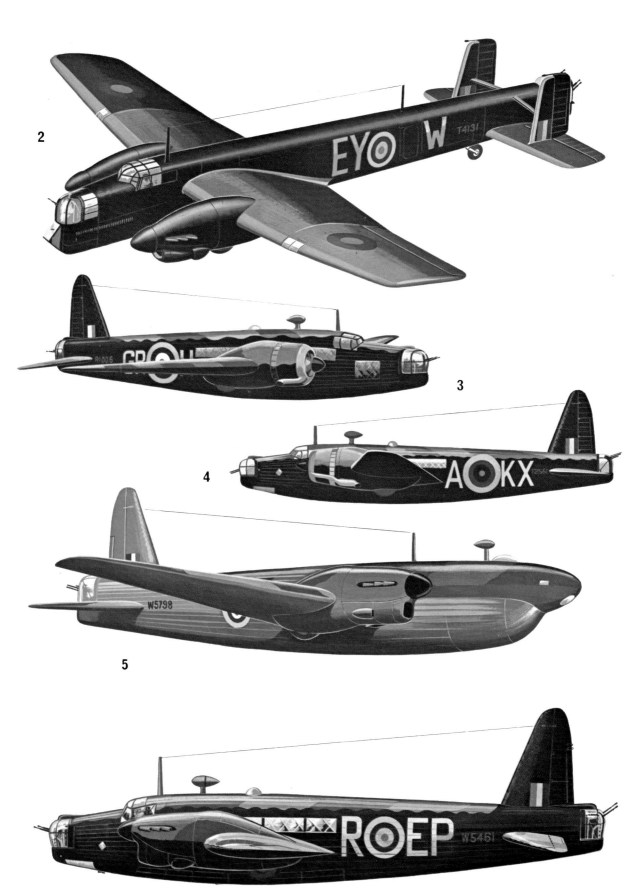

2

3

4

5

6

7

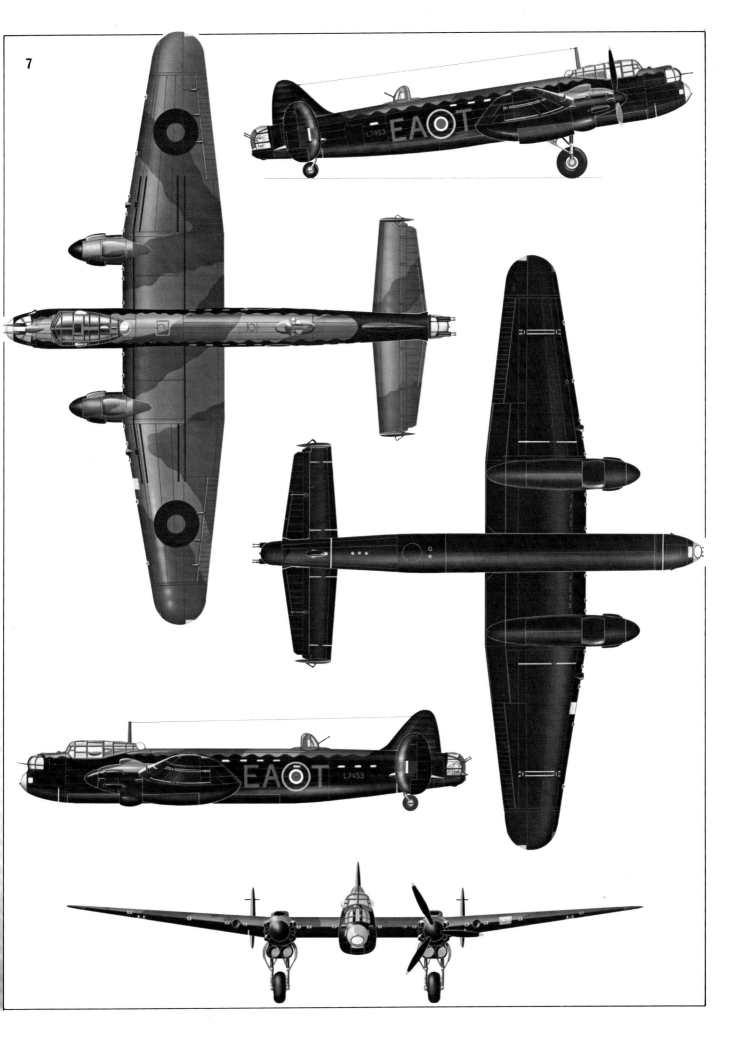

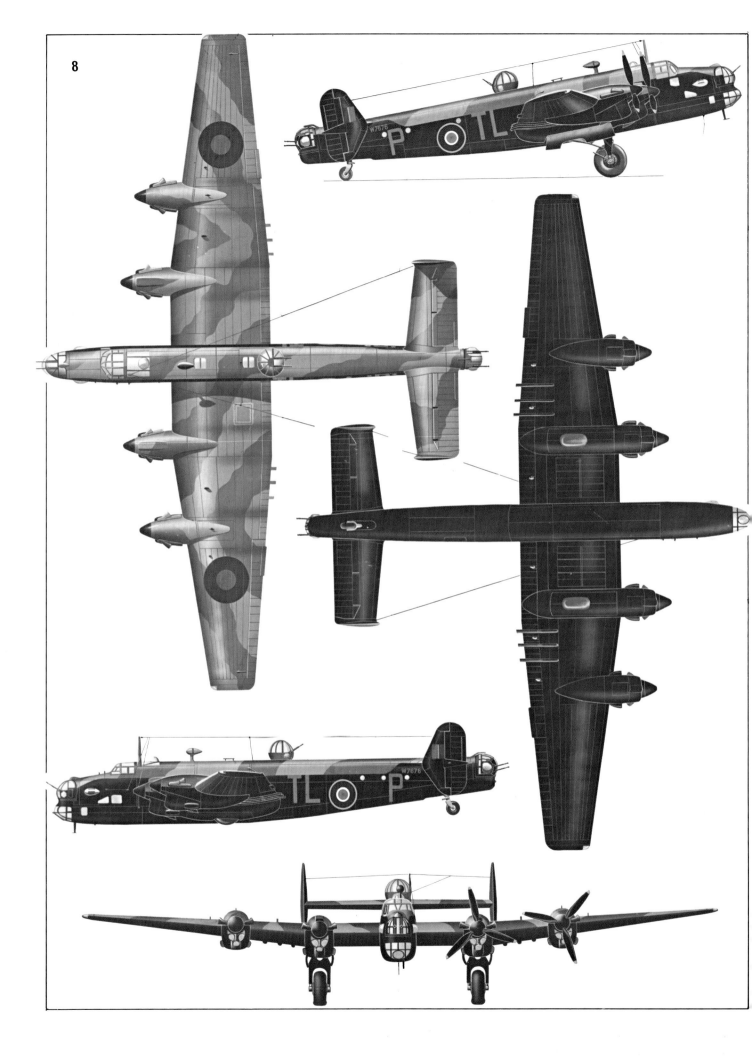

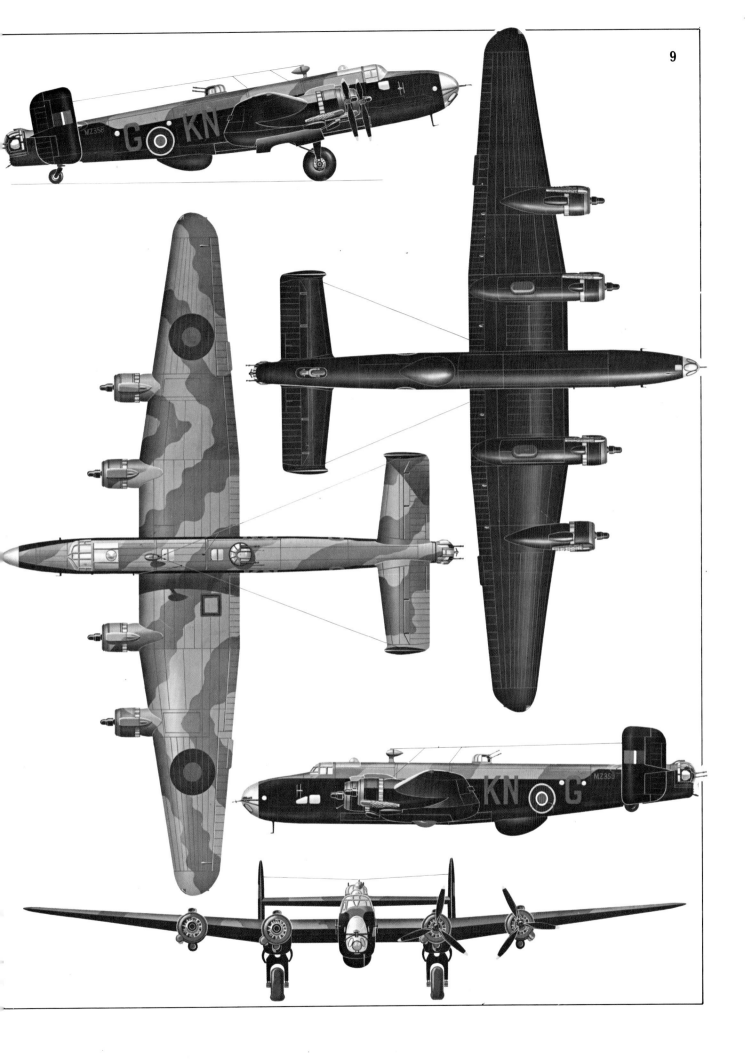

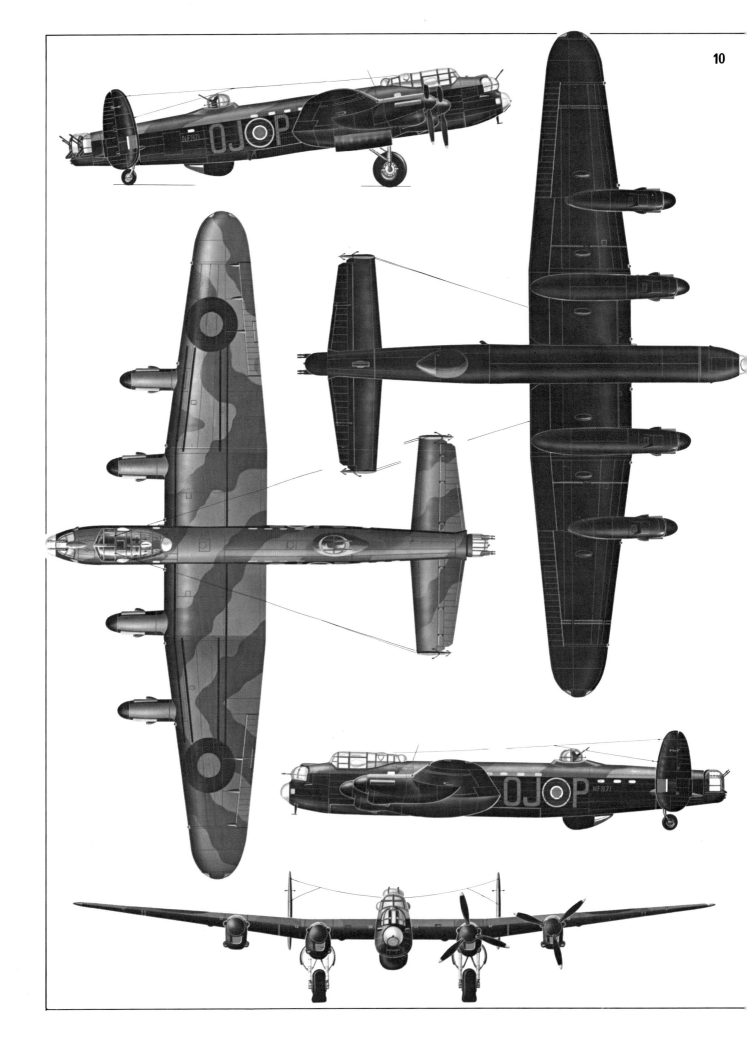

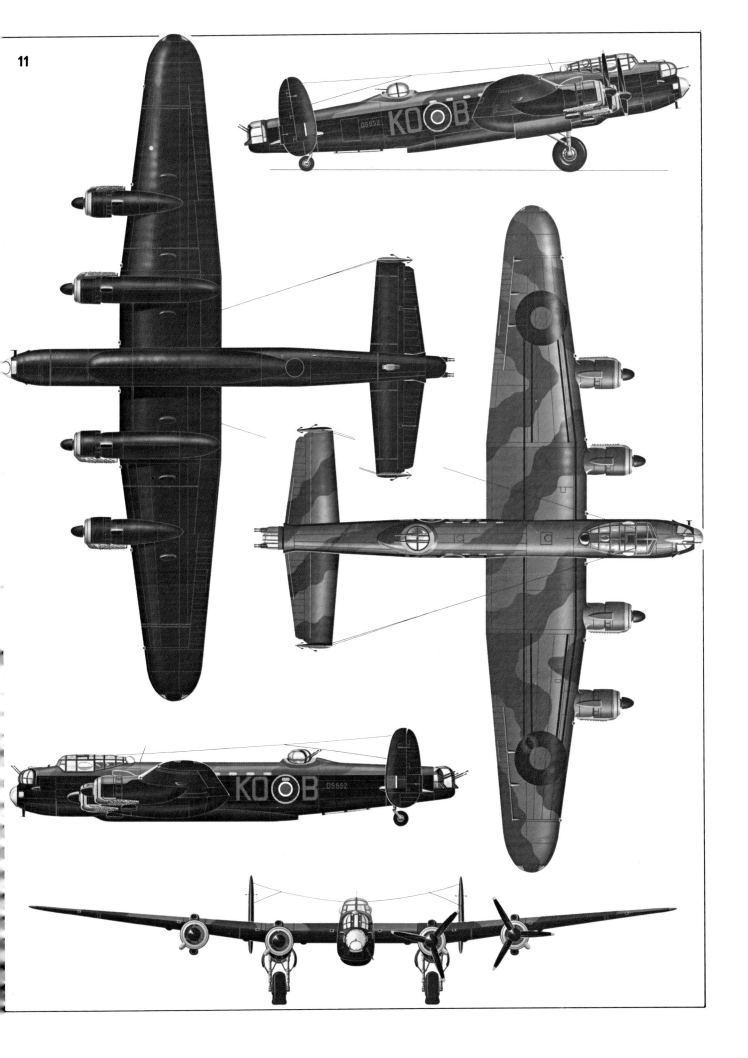

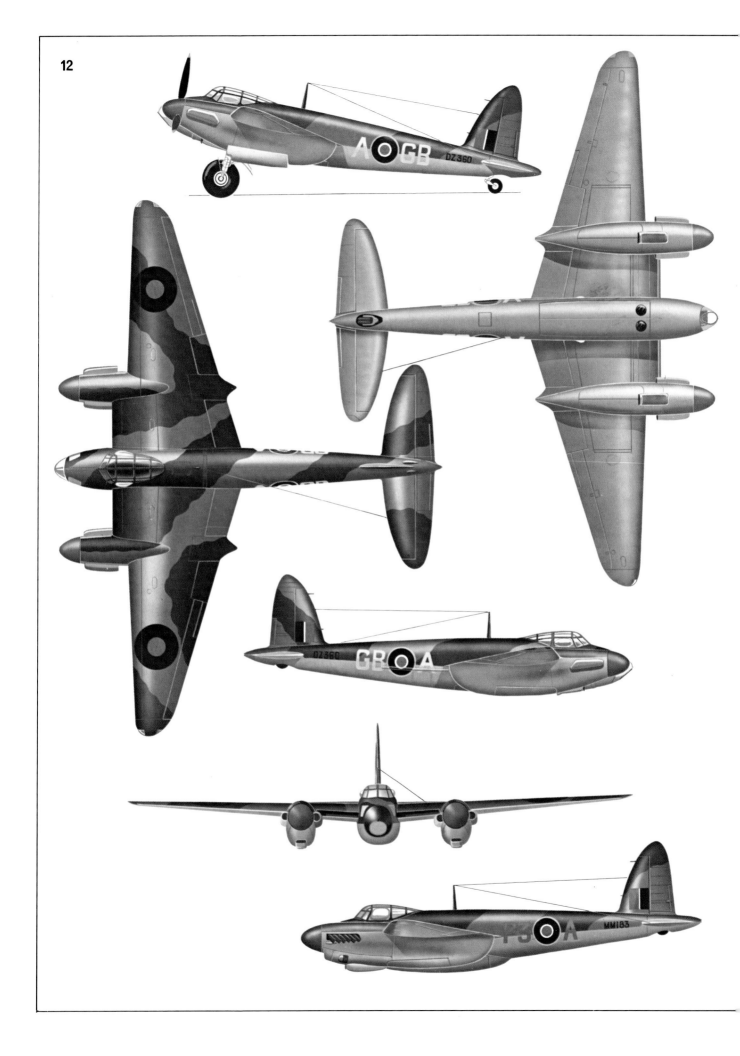

Above: Boeing Fortress III radio countermeasures aircraft of 100 Group. Overall Night finish on undersurfaces, Dark Green and Dark Earth on upper surfaces. In squadron service these aircraft were usually painted Night overall.

diameter over the Dull Blue ring, with a Dull Red centre of 21.5in diameter. The fuselage roundel was the standard Type C1 of 36in diameter, and the standard 24in × 24in fin flash was carried. Under wing roundels were not carried. Day-flying Mosquitoes carried the serial number in Night.

Special schemes

Early in 1941 90 Squadron began working-up on Boeing Fortress Is in preparation for high altitude bombing attacks against fringe targets in Northern Europe, and on 14 May 1941 the Air Ministry notified all commands that Fortress I bombers would have a special under surface finish for protection at high altitude in daylight. This would be applied to all under surfaces, up the fuselage sides and over the fins, and the colour would be a 'special sky blue'. Early in 1941 tests had been carried out at Boscombe Down on a Hurricane to develop a new colour for high-altitude operations. During these tests the under surface of one wing was painted with a 10 per cent lighter version of Azure Blue, while the under surface of the other wing was painted with a 10 per cent darker version. The Hurricane was then observed from another aircraft while flying at a height of around 30,000ft and more, and the resulting recommendation was that a colour 10 per cent darker than the darkest of the two blues tested, in effect 20 per cent darker than the standard Azure Blue, would be an exact match to the sky at those altitudes. This colour was given the official title of Deep Sky and was adopted as the standard colour for high-altitude bombers and for certain other special applications. The colour referred to in the Air Ministry notification as a 'special sky blue' was almost certainly Deep Sky.

The standard colour scheme for high altitude bombers was Dark Green and Dark Earth on upper surfaces and Deep Sky on under surfaces. This colour scheme was applied to Wellington Vs and Fortress Is, but the Wellington VI was intended to have Night under surfaces, presumably because it was intended solely for the night-bombing role in operational service. Many Wellington VIs were produced with Night under surfaces, but some were painted with Deep Sky under surfaces when they were used for special tests. It is thought that the Dark Green, Dark Earth and Deep Sky scheme was also applied to some Lancasters on special duties. Later in the war, the whole concept of really high altitude bombing was abandoned by the RAF because of technical problems involved in operating at heights of around 40,000ft, but the Mosquitos equipped with pressure cabins carried out raids at heights in the region of 30,000ft. These 'Mozzies', though, retained the standard finish of Dark Green, Ocean Grey and Medium Sea Grey, and had either Sky or Dull Red squadron code and aircraft letters. Some special Mosquito Mk IV bombers were modified to carry the 4,000lb 'cookie' high-capacity bomb and these, together with the Mk IVs and Mk IXs on *Oboe* operations, had the under surfaces, the fuselage sides and fins finished in Night, retaining the standard Dark Green and Ocean Grey on the upper surfaces. In these cases the squadron code and aircraft letters, and also the serials, were in Dull Red.

Another special colour scheme was that used on the Fortress IIs and IIIs and Liberator VIs of 215 Squadron and the Fortress IIs and IIIs of 223 Squadron operating on radio and radar countermeasures. These aircraft were painted overall in Night, with Dull Red squadron codes, aircraft letters and serials.

57

The Vickers Wellington

View of the Wellington IV prototype.

Although the Rolls-Royce Merlin-powered Wellington II began to enter squadron service in November 1940, the first to receive some being 12 Squadron at Binbrook followed closely by 142 Squadron at Driffield, it was not until April 1941 that it began operations. Only 12, 104 (later renumbered 158), 305 (Polish) and 405 (RCAF) Squadrons of Bomber Command were ever homogenous Wellington II units, but several other squadrons such as 99, 214 and 218 used a very small number alongside their radial-engined Wellingtons. As mentioned in Volume I, the Mk II was adapted to carry a 4,000lb bomb, and on the night of 31 March/1 April 1941 two Mk IIs, one each from 9 and 149 Squadrons, gave the enemy his first 'taste' of 'cookies' when they dropped two on Emden. The Wellington II, which, by the way, was the first mark to feature cabin heating and a 24-volt electrical system, continued in front-line service with Bomber Command until 1942, the last fully equipped user being 305 Squadron which finally relinquished it in August when it re-armed with the Wellington IV.

The next mark of Wellington was the Bristol-Hercules-engined Mk III, the prototype of which first flew, it will be remembered, in May 1939. This prototype was powered by Hercules HEISMs driving de Havilland constant speed propellers, but poor engine performance caused its development to be delayed. Eventually the engine problems were satisfactorily overcome, and with Hercules production assured Vickers were asked by the Air Ministry to convert a second airframe to take the new 1,425hp Hercules III, driving Rotol electric propellers. P9238, a Mk IC, was the airframe selected and it first flew with the new engine, which was built as a self-contained 'power-egg' including engine mounting, cowling, auxiliary drive and gearbox, in January 1941.

The production Wellington III was powered by 1,590hp Hercules XI engines, and although its all-up weight was 34,500lb, compared with 32,000lb for the Mk II and 30,000 for the Mks IA and IC, it was faster and had a greater range than the earlier marks. Max speed was 255mph at 12,500ft, service ceiling 19,500ft, and typical ranges and associated bomb loads were 2,200 miles with 1,500lb or 1,540 miles with 4,500lb.

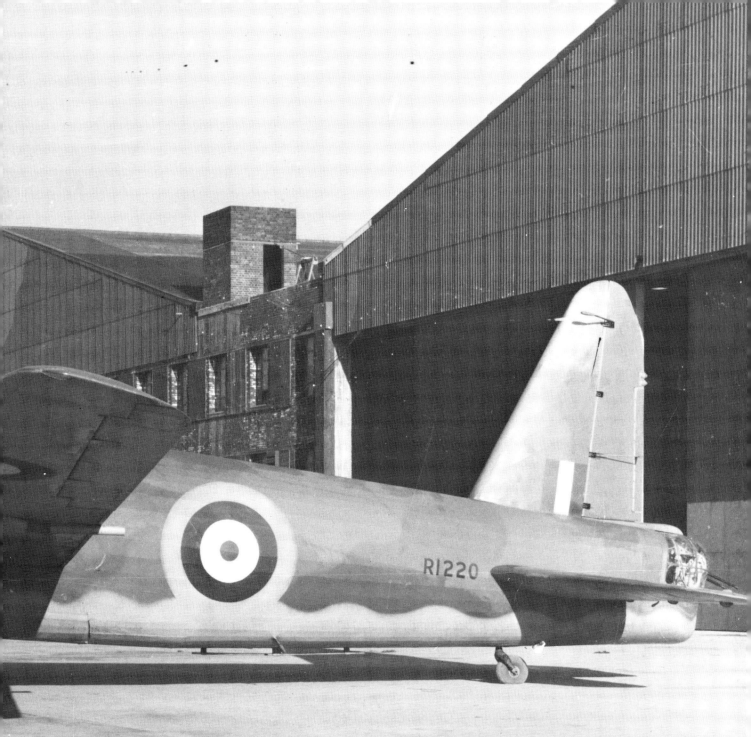

Following the bitter experience of late 1939, several schemes for improving the Wellington's defences against rear and beam attacks had been considered, including the fitting of a 20mm Hispano cannon rear turret and a low-drag Frazer-Nash ventral turret. The eventual choice was a four-gun Frazer-Nash rear turret and in March 1940 a trial installation was made in the Wellington III prototype L4251. It proved to be a success and was scheduled to be standard in the production Wellington III from the outset, but in the event deliveries were somewhat delayed and as a stop-gap the first Mk IIIs were fitted with the two-gun Frazer-Nash turret. Two other noteworthy features of the Mk III were bullet-proofed fuel tanks, barrage balloon cable cutters in the leading edges of the wing, and triangular windows incorporating beam-gun openings on each side of the rear fuselage.

Production of the Wellington III was handled by Vickers' shadow factories at Chester and Blackpool. The type began to reach 9 Squadron at Honington in June 1941 and in September this unit took it into action for the first time. Other 3 Group squadrons gradually received the 'Wimpy' III, and in 1942, as squadrons in other groups followed suit, it became Bomber Command's main version.

Built solely at Chester was the Wellington IV which was powered by Pratt & Whitney Twin Wasp R-1830 engines, originally ordered by France but not delivered due to that country's collapse. The prototype, a converted Mk IC serialled R1220, first flew in December 1940 and proved extremely noisy at high revs. The noise level was lowered eventually by replacing the original Hamilton propellers with Curtiss electric propellers. The prototype was to have been transferred from Chester to Weybridge for tests, but en route it suffered double engine failure due to carburettor icing and forced landed in the River Wey at Addlestone. However, a replacement airframe was readily available, which enabled a second Mk IV to be quickly produced and test flying to continue with the minimum of delay. Production of the Mk IV, which featured the four-gun rear turret of the Mk III, totalled 220 aircraft, all but the prototype being delivered between June 1941 and 1942.

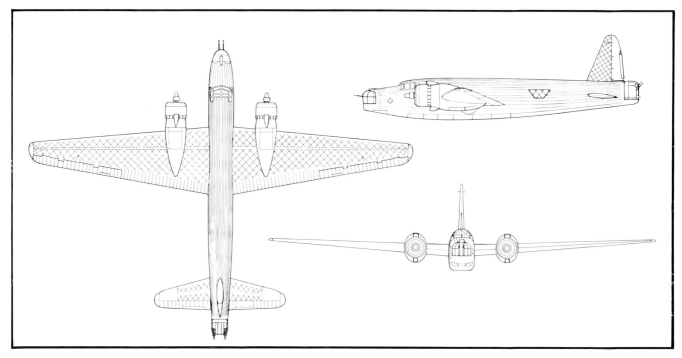

Deliveries to squadrons began in August 1941 to Nos 300 (Polish), 301 (Polish), and 458 (RAAF) Squadrons, after which 142, 460 (RAAF) and 305 (Polish) Squadrons also received them. The last-mentioned squadron received its Mk IVs in August 1942 and continued to use them until the following May, being the last to do so.

The Wellington V and VI high altitude bombers, whose beginnings have been covered in Vol I, will be dealt with again later on.

Next bomber mark was the VII, which was a Mk II re-engined with higher powered Merlin XXs. 150 were ordered in May 1941 and a prototype (T2545) flew, but the order was eventually cancelled.

Last, and best, of the Wellington bombers was the Mk X, which was developed from the III but had the higher-powered Hercules VI or XVI engines. Externally the only difference from the Mk III were the long carburettor air intakes atop the engine cowlings, but internally it was very different, the structure being 'beefed-up' for

higher gross weights by the use of newly developed light alloys equal in strength to mild steel. All-up weight of the Mk X was 36,500lb compared with the 34,500lb of the Mk III. It had the best performance of all Wellingtons and was the most numerous, production (all by Blackpool and Chester) totalling 3,803 aircraft. Serving as prototype Mk X was Blackpool-built Mk III X3374, and the first production machine, DF609 (also from Blackpool), flew in mid 1942. Main users in Bomber Command were the Canadian squadrons of 6 Group who found it a useful stop-gap between their ageing Mk IIIs and the Halifaxes and Lancasters which came later.

Bomber Command's last operational Wellington mission was

Above: Vickers Wellington B.Mk III.

Below: View of the Wellington IV prototype.

Above right: Beware the Moose. Wellington III Q-Queenie of the famous No 419 'Moose' Squadron, RCAF, which operated as part of the all-Canadian No 6 Bomber Group, pictured on test over Yorkshire.

flown by Mk Xs when, on 3/4 March 1944, aircraft of 300 (Polish) Squadron from Faldingworth laid mines off Lorient. Thus the 'Wimpy', which first went into action on the second day of the war, flew on ops with Bomber Command for exactly three and a half months, longer than either of its contemporaries, the Hampden and Whitley. At the peak period of its service with the Command, 21 Wellington squadrons were in the line, and in the first 1,000 bomber raid, on Cologne, more than half the force consisted of Wimpys, although some were supplied by Training Command.

When the time came for the bomber 'boys' to move on from the Wimpy to the four-engined heavies, many of them regretted the change, having developed a strong affection for their 'old cloth bombers'.

'Few aircraft', wrote one of them from 75 (New Zealand) Squadron, 'bore without serious complaint such continual increases in power, in all-up weight and armament as the Wellington during its various vicissitudes. As power and weight were piled on, the geodetics just stretched and took it happily. No other machine could feel quite like a Wellington in the air because always between the pilot and the result of his efforts there was a strange "something" which could only be described as flexibility. Everything waved quietly about and all the time one could feel a cross-section of the atmosphere. In bumpy weather the control column would move gently backwards and forwards while rear turret operation would produce strange movements of the rudder, the motors rocked slowly up and down and the wing tips waved in a miraculous rhythm. All the types of Wellingtons seemed to be nearly vice-free and they could be brought in to land at a ridiculously low speed. There were many occasions on which this was a decided advantage.'

Tributes to the Wimpy's ruggedness and ability to get home, time and again, seemingly 'on a wing and a prayer', abound in the RAF Forms 540s and 541s which jointly make up the squadron record books, but here just two examples will suffice. The first tale concerns Mk IC T2619 T-Tommy of 99 Squadron which took off from Waterbeach, Cambridgeshire, at 11.30pm on 14 July 1941 to attack an objective in Bremen. Its crew of six were all sergeants, the pilot being Sgt Saich, and it carried seven 500lb bombs.

The night was pitch dark and there was thick cloud, but just

before Bremen was reached the cloud gave way to a clear sky carved by the sharp beams of searchlights. There was a slight haze over the city 11,000ft below, but the target was located and the bombing run begun. One bomb was released when the wheeling searchlights caught and held T-Tommy in a cone of light, whereupon it came under the most intense and accurate barrage of both light and heavy flak. Two shells arrived, one bursting just behind and below the rear turret, the other inside the fuselage itself, level with the leading edge of the tailplane. The first shell wounded the rear gunner and cut the hydraulic controls to the turret, while fragments of the second shell set fire to the fabric covering the rear fuselage and the tail fin. T-Tommy quickly became a flying torch and attracted a storm of flak as a result. Saich took violent evasive action and succeeded in throwing the German gunners momentarily off their aim. Meanwhile the navigator went to help the rear gunner, whose turret he eventually reached after having subdued the flames in the rear fuselage with a fire extinguisher. The gunner had swung his turret round into the beam position to enable him to bale out by somersaulting backwards through the open turret doors. He was still in the turret but the doors now refused to close, so the navigator had to lean out through a hole beneath the fin, which he had just saved from burning, and, with the slipstream tearing at him, hack away at the steel doors with an axe until they fell off. The gunner was then able to rotate the turret manually, extricate himself and enter the fuselage.

While this was going on the Wimpy was hit again and flares carried in the port wing were set alight. They burned so brightly that Saich thought the port engine was on fire and he reacted by turning off its petrol, opening the throttle fully and switching off. Soon, however, the flames died down, for the flares had burnt their way through the fabric and fallen from the aircraft. Realising what had happened, Saich turned on the petrol and restarted the engine, while the second pilot crouched beside the main spar behind the wireless position and pumped all the oil which could be extracted from a riddled auxiliary tank. T-Tommy was still under intense flak fire and the shell splinters, one of which wounded the second pilot, were described by him as 'angry hail tearing through the aircraft'.

One further misfortune had befallen the Wellington. At the moment when it received its first hit, the bomb doors were open, for the aircraft was completing its first bombing run-up and one of the

bombs had just been released. The damage caused by the anti-aircraft shell was such as to make it impossible either to close the bomb doors or to release the remaining six bombs, since the hydraulic pipes had been punctured and the electrical wiring to the slips had been severed. In addition to this and the damage to the fuselage, the rear turret, the fin and the rudder, there was a large hole knocked by a shell in the starboard wing. It had just missed the petrol tanks. In this condition T-Tommy was headed for base, but the chances of making it looked slender. The aircraft was extremely difficult to control and Saich's task was not made easier by the hole in the wing through which the draught rushed, blanketing the starboard aileron which was for all intents and purposes useless. Nevertheless, he held doggedly to the homeward course given him by the navigator and at 5.35am on 15 July T-Tommy crossed the English coast dead on track. Its speed had been much reduced, and the petrol gauges had been registering zero gallons for some two hours out of the four on the return flight from Bremen, over nearly 300 miles of sea. The sky was now as 'pale as water before dawn' and Saich lost no time in selecting a barley field which looked suitable for an emergency landing. In the half light he did not see the obstruction poles set up in the field to hinder an airborne invasion and on touching down, with flaps up and only one mainwheel and the tailwheel extended, T-Tommy swung round, hit one of the poles and came abruptly to rest on its belly with its back

Above: Unusual head-on view of a Wellington VI high altitude, pressurised bomber in the air on test in February 1942. The pilot's head is just visible inside the domed cockpit hood behind which are the faired D/F loop and the wireless mast.

Below left: A Wellington IC of 149 Squadron with a 2,000lb armour-piercing bomb. / *IWM*

Above right: A new Wellington X displays the characteristic elongated air intakes of this mark atop its engine cowlings. Note the wide-bladed propellers to absorb the additional power provided by the Hercules XVI engines.

broken. It had flown to that East Anglian barley field with a gaping hole in its starboard wing, with innumerable smaller holes in its fuselage, with nine feet of fabric burned entirely away forward from the rear turret, and with half the fin and half the rudder in the same condition. For their good work in bringing T-Tommy home, Saich and his navigator, Sgt Smitten, were subsequently awarded the Distinguished Flying Medal.

The second 'wing and a prayer' episode concerns a Wellington IC of 103 Squadron from Elsham Wolds, captained by 20-year old Flt Lt Clive Saxelby, a New Zealander, during the 1,000 bomber raid on Cologne in May 1942. It had bombed the target and had crossed the Dutch/German frontier on the way home when a German fighter attacked it. The second pilot was killed immediately, the fuselage set on fire, and rear turret shattered and the gunner wounded. The undercarriage swung down and the bomb doors fell open. To add to Saxelby's difficulties, an oxygen tube in the fuselage caught fire and filled the fuselage with choking fumes. The Wimpy began to lose height, but Saxelby, although hardly able to see, eventually managed to get it under control. Then came another attack by a German fighter, and only by diving almost to ground level did Saxelby finally manage to shake it off. He then completed the difficult return flight to England in the rather skeletal bomber and force-landed at Honington. During an earlier raid Saxelby had had a somewhat unusual and harrowing experience when an incendiary bomb from another British aircraft fell into one of his engines and started a fire. This attracted the enemy gunners but, by running the engine dry, the fire was subdued and the aircraft got clear.

High-altitude Wellington VI

Because flight trials of the Wellington V high altitude bomber (Vol I, page 100) revealed that the power output was below expectation, only one production model (W5796) was fully completed, production concentrating instead on the Merlin 60-powered Mk VI. The prototype of the latter (W5795) was produced from one of several completed Mk V airframes that never actually had Hercules engines fitted, and at one stage its wing span was increased by 12ft. W5795 first flew at Weybridge in 1941 and was afterwards flown to the A & AEE at Boscombe Down for evaluation and, finally, to Rolls-Royce's test establishment at Hucknall, Notts, for further development trials.

Like its Hercules-powered predecessor, the Mk VI was made capable of partial pressurisation by the installation in the upper part of the front fuselage of what amounted to a vast steel boiler housing the entire crew of four — pilot, navigator, bomb aimer and wireless operator. A shallow double Perspex dome was installed above the pilot's seat, enabling him to see out. It was a continual source of trouble: the oil mist introduced by the cabin blowers into the pressure cabin frosted over the dome's inner surface at heights above 20,000ft. This meant instrument flying until the aircraft descended into warmer air or, alternatively, constant use of the pilot's thumbnail to scrape off the frost.

The Mk VI prototype did, in fact, reach 40,000ft during its trials, and although the temperatures down to -70°C caused several serious problems, all of them, including the one already mentioned, were eventually overcome. At first it was intended that a pressurised Frazer Nash 4 x .303in gun rear turret should be installed in the Wellington VI, but as this was not available in time a remotely controlled Frazer Nash turret using periscopic sighting was substituted. Altogether, 64 Mk VIs were produced including 18 re-engined Mk Vs — assembly and test flying taking place at Vickers' wartime facility at Smiths Lawn in Windsor Great Park. Several variants of the Mk VI existed, but as these have already been dealt with in detail in Alec Lumsden's book *Wellington Special* (Ian Allan, 1975) it is not necessary to describe them here. All that need be said here is that the two main ones were the VIA (27 production aircraft all being Mk V airframes converted to

Merlins) and the VIG (32 production aircraft with *Oboe,* three of them trainers). The remaining three were Mk VIs built as such from the outset, and two of these had provision for stowage of a 4,000lb bomb.

The American Sperry bomb sight was installed in the nose of the Mk VI, an optically flat window, inclined at about 30 degrees to the line of flight, being provided for the bomb aimer. Rectangular windows — double glazed and supplied with hot air de-misting and de-frosting like the pilot's canopy — were located along the top of the cabin to enable the navigator to take sextant readings. Loaded weight of the Wellington VI was 30,450lb, max speed at operational height 300mph, normal range 1,510 miles, max range 2,180 miles, ceiling 38,500ft (40,000ft with extended wings — fitted temporarily to the prototype and also Mk VIA W5800 only), and bomb load 4,500lb.

The Mk VIs were all delivered to the RAF between May 1942 and March 1943 but most of them languished in maintenance units until they were scrapped. Two Mk VIAs, W5801 and W5802, did, however, find their way to 109 Squadron, then a radio countermeasures trials unit, at Stradishall, Suffolk, in March 1942 for experimental use. W5802 was transferred to the RAE in May, but W5801 remained at Stradishall until July and is thought to have made at least two sorties over Germany in daylight. In December 1942 and January 1943 two Mk VIGs, DR481 and DR485, served with 109 Squadron, but although the Mk VI in this *Oboe*-equipped form had possibilities as a target marker, it was by now completely outclassed by the Mosquito.

Among those who tested the Mk VI while it was with 109 Squadron was Air Vice Marshal D. C. T. Bennett, AOC the Pathfinder Force, and in his autobiography *Pathfinder* (Frederick Muller, 1958) he described how his single flight caused him no small amount of trouble. Due to an unhappy incident following the discovery of an air leak in the pressure cabin, the air pressure changed from the equivalent of about 6,000 or 8,000ft to 30,000ft in a split second, after which the process was reversed for some 20 or 30 seconds. Bennett was suffering from a very bad cold in the head at the time, and the result was internal infection of both ears, which made the next 10 days very unpleasant for him.

The Short Stirling

Although formed at Leeming, Yorkshire, a station in 4 Group, the first Stirling Squadron, No 7, officially transferred to Oakington, Cambridgeshire, in 3 Group in October 1940; however, several weeks elapsed before any Stirlings actually arrived there. Initially, at Leeming, the Stirlings had twin-Browning retractable dustbin turrets of Frazer-Nash design, but these proved too cramped for continuous occupation and, in addition to increasing drag when lowered in flight, had a habit of slipping down through leakage of the hydraulic non-return valves when vibrated during taxying, causing the guns to scrape along the ground. These turrets were therefore removed and the early production Stirling B.Mk Is were fitted with single pivoted Browning guns firing through side windows. Later, twin beam guns became standard, but these proved inadequate in combat with the result that they, in turn, were

replaced by a Frazer-Nash dorsal turret similar to that of the Avro Manchester; the new turrets appeared on Stirling Is supplied to 7 Squadron in June 1941.

No 7 flew its first operational Stirling sorties on the night of 10/11 January 1941, when three aircraft dropped a total of 46 500lb bombs on oil storage tanks at Rotterdam. Three months later 15 Squadron at Wyton also received Stirlings and by the year end more than 150 Stirlings had been delivered to the RAF and a third squadron, No 149 at Mildenhall, was operational. Gradually, as other 3 Group squadrons converted from Wellingtons to Stirlings, the Short bomber became the group's standard equipment. The Stirlings were often operated by day as well as by night during 1941, their first day raid being against Emden on 27 April.

In a day raid on the *Scharnhorst* at La Pallice in the afternoon of

First squadron to receive Stirlings was No 7 Squadron, one of whose original machines is shown. / *British Official*

23 July, one of two Stirlings of 15 Squadron which reached the target area was attacked by German fighters and had to be ditched in the sea. Three aircraft of 7 Squadron also reached the target area and a 2,000lb bomb from one of these scored a direct hit on the stern of the *Scharnhorst* from 13,000ft. This same Stirling, N6037, was attacked by two Bf109s but both were shot down by the rear gunner.

The Stirling was extremely agile, largely due to its low aspect ratio wing (6.5) and powerful elevators, and despite its limited ceiling, about 18,000ft, again due to the low aspect ratio, it was popular with its crews. Another of its attributes was its ability to sustain damage and still keep flying. An excellent example of this was seen on 27/28 June 1942, when Stirling I N3751 of 214 Squadron, from Stradishall, took part in a raid on Bremen.

The Stirling, captained by Sgt F. M. Griggs, an Australian, had bombed the target and was crossing the Dutch frontier on its way home when two twin-engined 'twin-tailed' fighters, apparently Bf110s, attacked simultaneously. The bomber's front and mid-upper gunners retaliated and one night fighter was driven off and the other shot down and seen to crash. During this phase, the Stirling had one engine, its intercomm, radio and electrical systems put out of action, the rear gunner was killed and the wireless operator wounded. Griggs struggled to keep his damaged aircraft on course but as he crossed the Dutch coast his navigator spotted two Bf109s diving to attack. The front gunner, who was giving first aid to the w/op was barely warned in time by the navigator, who had to run down the fuselage to give the alarm. Both 109s were shot down into the sea, but the Stirling had taken still more punishment and had dropped to 8,000ft where flak ships found it an easy target. Soon afterwards another 109 attacked and in manoeuvring to escape from it Griggs lost control of his crippled bomber which began to dive. He was almost at sea level when he regained flying attitude and struggled across the North Sea on his three remaining engines. Above the airfield a second engine caught fire, but the flames were extinguished and with only the two port engines working Griggs managed to crash-land without injuring any member of the crew.

During the opening raid of the Battle of Hamburg in July 1943, a Stirling of 75 (New Zealand) Squadron even survived a head-on mid-air collision with a Bf109. Four feet of the Stirling's starboard wing was torn away and the bomber plunged for 300ft before the pilot, Flg Off G. Turner, regained control. He and his co-pilot found that they could only keep the Stirling level by pushing the control column hard over to port. In this fashion they set course for home. After about half an hour both their arms and legs were aching with the strain and for the remainder of the two-hour flight they lashed the control column over with parachute elastic.

In August 1942 No 7 Squadron was chosen, with three other squadrons (not flying Stirlings), to form the nucleus of the Path Finder Force and was soon helping to lead main force squadrons as far afield as Genoa, Turin and Milan in northern Italy. On one raid against Turin the weather was so bad that only two Stirlings out of the eight detailed from 7 Squadron reached their objective. In the vicinity of the Alps the cloud bank was over 20,000ft, and the two Stirlings flew through it on dead reckoning to emerge almost directly over Turin. Only the aircraft piloted by Flt Lt J. F. Barron, a New Zealander, completed its mission, the other being shot down over the target. During a subsequent raid on Munich Barron's Stirling was twice attacked by night fighters. The rear gunner drove one off and probably destroyed it, but the other, a Ju88, made

repeated attacks, raking the bomber with machine-gun fire. Parts of the wing and tailplane were torn away and the fuel supply so damaged that both port engines threatened to stop through lack of petrol. Eventually, the flight engineer improvised repairs that enabled the Stirling to limp home.

Shortly afterwards, in a raid on Hamburg, Barron had one of the engines shot from his aircraft whilst over the target. During the return flight the Stirling ran into a storm and ice began to form on the wings and fuselage. With only three engines it was unable to climb above the cloud, and it was gradually forced lower and lower until, over Rotterdam, it was at barely 2,000ft. The crew furiously jettisoned guns, ammunition, and everything else they could to lighten the bomber. Finally, just as they were preparing to bale out, the ice began to melt and Barron was able to gain sufficient height to get home safely.

At the beginning of 1943 some of 7 Squadron's Stirlings, together with some Halifaxes of 35 (PFF) Squadron, had been fitted with *H2S* radar and on the 30/31 January the two squadrons pioneered the operational use of the device in a raid on Hamburg. Three nights later, when Bomber Command made its next *H2S* attack against Cologne, one of No 7's *H2S* aircraft was shot down near Rotterdam in Holland by a German fighter with the result that the enemy captured some of the top secret radar equipment and was able to start probing its secrets.

By now the bomber streams were having to fly ever increasingly higher on their nightly forays in order to evade the more powerful anti-aircraft fire; as this happened the Stirling gradually lost its

Below: A Stirling I of No 149 Squadron takes off from its base at Mildenhall, Suffolk, in the winter of 1941/42.

Above right: Stirling wings and fuselages on the production line at Austin Motors' Longbridge, Birmingham, works. Large holes cut out of the top surfaces of the wings are for the installation of fuel tanks.

popularity with its crews, for it was unable to fly at more than 18,000ft when fully loaded with bombs, and indeed it was often hard put to reach 12,000. On the long range trips to Italy the terrain clearance across the Alps was often only marginal and many pilots must have stories to tell of how they went *through* the Alps instead of over them.

Apart from its poor ceiling, the Stirling was always handicapped by its inability to carry any bombs larger than 2,000 pounders and its exceptionally long undercarriage which made it difficult to handle near the ground. A further source of trouble were the exactor controls, hydraulic devices which worked the throttles. They suffered considerably from air bubbles and it was not unknown for a full movement of throttle levers to be made without changing the note of the engines.

Arrangements to build Stirlings in Canada were made in 1941 and a contract was placed for 140 Stirling B.Mk IIs powered by 1,600hp Wright Cyclone R-2600-A5B engines. Two Mk II prototypes were produced at Rochester by converting Mk Is N3657 and N3711 and flown in August and December 1941, but soon afterwards the Canadian contract was cancelled and the Mk II never entered production. Further projected production of the Mk II at the South Marston (Wilts) shadow factory, which was already producing the Mk I, was also abandoned.

A third and final bomber mark of Stirling appeared in 1942, the B.Mk III (1,635hp Hercules XVI engines with underslung oil coolers), the prototypes of which were converted from Mk Is R9188 and R9309. The B.III was generally similar to the B.I Srs III (which, unlike the B.I Srs I and II, had complete Bristol-

designed power-plant assemblies on 'power-eggs' including oil tanks and engine-driven accessories), minor differences being the installation of a Lancaster-type FN50 dorsal turret (also seen on some Mk I Srs IIIs), larger fuel tanks, and a revised interior layout with fewer oval windows in the rear fuselage. The B.III weighed 43,200lb empty and had a max all-up weight of 70,000lb. Max speed was 270mph at 14,500ft, normal cruising speed 200mph at 15,000ft and service ceiling 18,000ft. It could fly 2,010 miles with 3,500lb of bombs or 590 miles with 14,000lb. Stirling B.III production was undertaken at Rochester, South Marston, Belfast and the Austin shadow factory at Longbridge (Birmingham), all of whom had previously built the Mk I. Stirling IIIs re-equipped existing Stirling squadrons, not always completely, by any means, and were also issued to five new squadrons which formed in 3 Group during the summer of 1943.

Already, however, the Stirling was on the wane, being completely outclassed by the Lancaster, and from late 1943 rising casualties resulted in it being allotted only the less difficult targets including the V-weapon sites which the Germans were building in northern France. Simultaneously it was relegated extensively to minelaying and supply dropping to the French Resistance movement. Stirlings of the main force last flew as bombers on 8 September 1944, when 149 Squadron bombed Le Havre, but 199 Squadron, which had been transferred to 100 (Bomber Support) Group in May of that year, continued to fly them until mid-March 1945, its 'spoof' work sometimes including diversionary bombing attacks as well as radio and radar jamming. For this special role its Stirling IIIs were equipped with various RCM devices including *Mandrel*, which

countered the German *Freya* early warning radar, and were readily distinguishable at close quarters by the profusion of aerials projecting from the undersides of their fuselages.

Altogether, Stirlings operating with Bomber Command flew a total of 18,440 operational sorties on bombing, mining and other duties, dropped 27,821 tons of bombs and laid a large number of mines in enemy water. Aircraft losses, from all causes, totalled 769, of which 606 were classified 'missing'.

The successful laying of mines depended on aircraft flying in low to the dropping point, not only to achieve accuracy but also to avoid exploding the mines by the shock of impact, which was likely to occur if they were dropped from more than 1,000ft. This of course meant that the chance of interception and the dangers from flak were greater than might have been the case had they been able to drop their mines from higher levels, and indeed casualties were relatively heavy. An example of the many 'dicey do's' experienced by 3 Group Stirlings on minelaying sorties was that of 18/19 January 1943, involving Sgt R. F. Bennett's aircraft of 75 Squadron, one of two from the New Zealand squadron sent to lay mines in the Gironde estuary.

Above left: A brand new Stirling III. In the latter part of the war these aircraft were extensively used for minelaying and some ended their operational service in the radio countermeasures role.

Below left: This view of a Stirling being bombed-up well illustrates the way in which the fuselage bomb bay was divided into three narrow compartments, a feature which prevented the bomber from carrying anything bigger than 2,000lb bombs, which latter are not shown here. / *British Official*

Below: Incendiary bomb containers arrive at the dispersal point of a Stirling I of No 218 Squadron at Marham, Norfolk. / *British Official*

As it neared the French coast the Stirling was attacked by a Bf110 but, before it could do any damage the mid-upper and rear gunners had both fired short bursts, upon which the 110 pulled over on to its back. The Stirling laid its mines in the estuary, but on the way out it passed over several German flak ships. These put up an intense barrage, rocking the aircarft, but it managed to get clear. No sooner had a course been set for base when a Ju88 was sighted to port. Bennett took evasive action but the fighter hung on without opening fire. Describing this incident later, Bennett said:

'The reason for this soon became obvious when my rear gunner gave me directions for turning away from another Junkers from the rear. Each German fighter appeared to be acting as a decoy for the other. Had I adopted my rear gunner's direction we should have been exposed to the fire of the fighter on our port wing.'

The rear and mid-upper gunners were able to get in bursts at the enemy on their tail, who was so close that when he returned fire the gunners could actually hear the noise of the German cannon. The Stirling was almost down to sea level by now and must have been silhouetted against the reflection of the moon, making it a sitting duck for the enemy.

But luck was on their side, for a thick blanket of cloud suddenly appeared and gave the Stirling protection, the fighters being lost. A course was again set for base but once more the crew found themselves over the flak ships; however, they soon got clear. The action had been so violent that everything movable in the Stirling had been thrown on to the floor and the navigator, who had been sitting behind the pilot, retrieved his maps from well forward of the bomb-sight, down in the nose of the aircraft.

The Handley Page Halifax

The Handley Page HP57 Halifax began operations in March 1941 with 35 Squadron based at Linton-on-Ouse, in 4 Group, as already mentioned (together with its early teething troubles). Two nights after their initial foray against Le Havre, the new heavies raided Hamburg and in so doing became the first British four-engined bombers to bomb a target in Germany.

Defensive armament of the Halifax B.I consisted of nose and tail Boulton-Paul power-operated turrets, mounting two and four .303in Browning guns respectively, these being supplemented at first by single .303in beam guns which poked out through special hatches.

Not until July 1941 did the British public at large learn of the Halifax's existence. The announcement followed a successful attack on the notorious *Scharnhorst* at La Pallice. The German

battlecruiser had slipped out of Brest but two direct hits and a hot time in general compelled her to return. She remained in Brest until an escape with the *Gneisenau* enabled them both to regain their home ports in a very battered condition.

The Halifax was withdrawn from daylight operations after a final raid on the two warships at Brest at the end of 1941. Although its ability to withstand extensive battle damage and return to base had been amply proved, increasing fighter opposition had threatened to make the casualty rate in daylight raids prohibitive.

Analysis of early air combats at night by the Operational Research Section of Bomber Command showed that the Halifax's beam guns were rarely used, whereas the rear gunner often had a very hectic time dealing with enemy fighters employing their favourite tactic of climbing up out of the darkness on to the

bomber's tail. So the beam guns were removed and a new Boulton-Paul two-gun dorsal turret of the type used on the Lockheed Hudson was installed instead. This boosted fire power in the rear to six guns and proved quite effective. Simultaneously, four of the new 1,175hp Merlin XX or XXII engines were fitted, and so was born the Halifax B.II Series I. The .303in Browning gun was to remain the standard defensive armament of all our big operational bombers throughout World War II and this policy of the Air Ministry has

A Halixfax B.II Srs I (Special) in the markings of 10 Squadron, a unit of 4 Group, which operated during the latter part of the war from Melbourne, Yorkshire. / *Aeroplane*

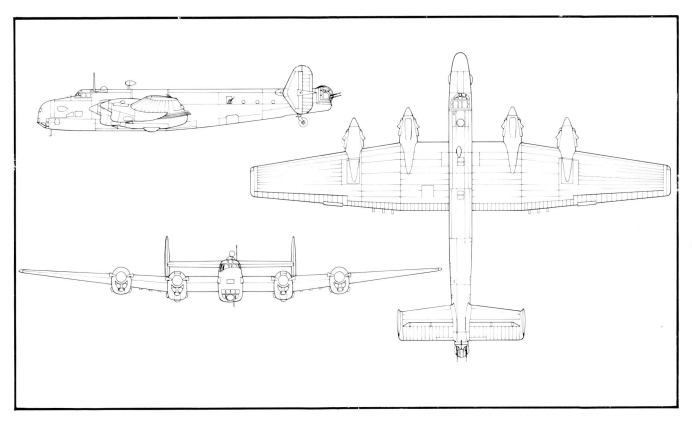

Above left: Making an interesting comparison with the II Srs I (Special) is this shot of a Halifax II Srs IA of 78 Squadron from RAF Breighton, near Selby, Yorks, in the late summer of 1943. Note the Perspex nose, Defiant-type dorsal turret and 'square' fins and rudders. /*IWM*

Below left: The second prototype Halifax in flight over the A&AEE, Boscombe Down. /*Aeroplane*

Above: Handley Page Halifax B.Mk II Series I (Special). This aircraft had the front and mid-upper turrets removed to increase performance.

always been the subject of much controversy. Certainly the .303in 'peashooters' as they have been scathingly dubbed by the critics, were no match for the standard cannon armament of the German fighters, but they *were* light, enabling a maximum bomb load to be carried, their turrets were in quantitiy production, and night fighting usually took place at close quarters. They were, in fact, much more effective than many critics claimed, and our heavies claimed a considerable number of enemy fighters at night. Several Halifax gunners in particular ran up quite notable tallies of enemy fighters, two names which come to mind being Sgt Porritt of 10 Squadron, and Sgt P. Engbrecht of 424 'Tiger' Squadron, RCAF. In a raid on the military rehabilitation camp at Bourg Leopold on the night of 27/28 May 1944, Engbrecht, who was mid-upper gunner for Flt Lt O. J. G. Keys, USAAF, using the four-gun dorsal turret armament of his Halifax Mk III (of which more later) shot down a Fw190 and a Messerschmitt Bf110 while beating off no less than 14 attacks. The 190 blew up in the air while the 110 exploded as it hit the ground. During a raid on Versailles-Matelots the following month, Engbrecht scored another double when, with the help of Sgt C. C. Gillanders, the rear gunner in Flt Lt Key's Halifax, he shot down a Bf109 and a Bf110. For this and the general excellence of his record, Engbrecht was awarded the Conspicuous Gallantry Medal and later commissioned. On the night of 12/13 August 1944 when the Tiger Squadron bombed Falaise in an effort to harass the Germans attempting to escape encirclement by Allied troops, this same redoubtable pair downed an Me410 and a Bf109, both of

which burst into flames and exploded. Gillanders was awarded the DFM and four nights later he claimed a probable.

These scores were certainly unusually high but they do go to show that in the hands of good sharp-shooters like Engbrecht and Gillanders, the .303in Brownings were quite capable of claiming a good toll of enemy fighters, despite the latter's superior cannon armament.

But to get back to the early Halifaxes. Operational experience with the Halifax B.II Srs I showed that its bulky and weighty dorsal turret and its almost equally cumbersome nose turret produced so much drag that they were a serious handicap to performance. As a result, the B.Mk II Series I (Special) had no dorsal turret, at least not initially, and, instead of a nose turret, it featured a so-called Z-type metal fairing. Also absent were the six fuel-jettison pipes which had hitherto extended aft of the trailing edge of the wing. The B.II Srs I (Special) played a prominent part in the big Battles of the Ruhr and Hamburg in 1943, but it was only an interim version, for there appeared, during the summer, the B.II Srs IA, which had a low-drag Boulton-Paul Defiant-type four-gun dorsal turret (also fitted to late B.II Srs I (Special) aircraft) and a neat, moulded Perspex nose mounting a single hand-operated Vickers K gun. Powered by Merlin XXIs or XXIIs, this cleaned-up Halifax had an edge of about 20mph in cruising speed on the earlier versions. Range with 4,000lb of bombs was 1,900 miles, and with 13,000lb of bombs it was 600 miles. Maximum speed was 260mph at 19,000ft and service ceiling 21,000ft.

To overcome a shortage of Messier undercarriages, the Halifax V, using a Dowty lever suspension undercarriage, was also introduced in 1943; the two main versions, Mk V Srs I (Special) and Srs IA, corresponded to the Mk II variants. Some Mk II Srs IAs and Mk V Srs IAs were fitted with *H2S* in a ventral blister, or alternatively a ventral gun position mounting a single 0.5in Browning gun. The latter was an attempt to counter enemy night fighters who, realising that the bombers were extremely vulnerable to attack from astern and below, claimed most of their victims in this way. The Halifax casualty rate had invariably been much

heavier than that of the Lancaster on account of the Handley Page bomber's inferior speed and operational ceiling, and even with the introduction of the B.II and V variants the Halifax continued to suffer throughout 1943. It was not until February 1944, when the Bristol Hercules-powered Mk III became available in quantity, that the Halifax began, in the words of Sir Arthur Harris' despatch on the bombing offensive, 'to hold its own against the formidable fighter defences of the Reich.'

In addition to its heavy operational casualty rate, the Halifax was more accident-prone than the Lancaster. There were many fatal crashes, largely due to rudder stall, although for a long time the cause remained a mystery. When it was finally traced the trouble was soon cured by replacing the small triangular fin with the large 'square' one which became part of the Halifax recognition 'trade mark.'

Before leaving the Merlin Halifax, mention must be made of the B.II Srs II, a one-off prototype made by installing Merlin 65s driving four-bladed propellers in a production Mk II Srs IA (HR756) and extending the inboard nacelles. These modifications were to have been features of the projected HP 60 Halifax B.IV which did not enter production. A further derivative of this modification would have been the HP 60A, designed to Specification B.1/39, but only built in mock-up form.

In 1943 Handley Page re-engined a 'hack' Halifax II (R9534) with 1,615hp Bristol Hercules VI radial engines, and tests with this aircraft led to the Halifax B.III which had the type number HP 61.

Above left: Brand new Halifax IIIs at Handley Page's airfield at Radlett. Empty weight of this mark was 38,900lb, and maximum all-up weight 65,000lb.

Below left: Of interest in this picture of a 425 'Alouette' Squadron Halifax III of the RCAF's own bomber group, 6 Group, is the ventral gun position mounting a single .303in Browning gun. / *RCAF*

Above right: Nose of Halifax B.III Y-Yorker of 51 Squadron after the mid-air collision described in the text. / *Philip J. R. Moyes collection*

Hercules XVI engines of 1650hp each were installed in the production Mk III aircraft, and in addition to improving the bomber's performance they allowed its all-up weight to be increased to 65,000lb. The first-off, HX226, flew in July 1943, and during the type's production run its wing span was increased from 98ft 10in to 104ft 2in. The increase in wing area improved the operational ceiling, and the extended, curved tips became standard on all subsequent marks. Other features included a retractable tailwheel (previously introduced on the Mk I but abandoned) and a ventral 0.5in Browning-armed gun position, though the latter was more usually replaced by decidedly offensive equipment in the form of an *H2S* radar scanner. Maximum speed of the B.III was 280mph at 13,500ft, and service ceiling was 20,000ft. It had a range of 1,985 miles with 7,000lb of bombs, or 1,030 miles with 13,000lb of bombs.

The B.III entered service in November 1943, beginning with 433 (RCAF) and 466 (RAAF) Squadrons, and by the year's end several squadrons of both 4 and 6 Groups were operating it. During the next few months the Command's Merlin-engined Halifaxes were completely replaced by the Mk III, the change-over being completed in July 1944 when 347 (Free French Air Force) Squadron at Elvington was re-equipped.

Many were the occasions when the Halifax proved its ability to withstand heavy damage and still get home safely. One such example was seen in April 1944 when B.III K-King of 433 'Porcupine' Squadron, RCAF, landed at the emergency airfield at Woodbridge, in Suffolk, after a raid on Karlsruhe, with 64 square feet of its starboard wing showing daylight and with its navigational equipment shot to pieces by flak. Two months later, C-Charlie of the same squadron managed to struggle back to England from Metz with the starboard fin and rudder shot off, the starboard elevator, aileron and wing smashed, and the starboard flap and wing badly damaged; furthermore, for most of the journey it flew on three engines.

Apart from the hazards of enemy flak and fighters, the aircraft of Bomber Command always had to face the possibility of being struck by falling bombs or even a collision with a bomber itself. It was the result of such a mid-air collision that B.III Y-Yorker (MZ465) of 51 Squadron, from Snaith, near Selby, became legendary in 4 Group by returning to England minus its entire nose and with only three of its instruments working. The collision occurred during a raid on Saarbrücken on 13/14 January 1945; another Halifax crossed its path and sliced off Yorker's nose with its tail, the luckless navigator and the bomb aimer, neither of whom were wearing their parachutes at the time, falling out. Fortunately, Yorker's engines continued to function perfectly, although the propellers were dented, probably by bits of wreckage which shook loose and flew off the fuselage. Some of the skin on the nose was bent round and gave the remaining crew some protection against the wind which whistled through the bomber as it flew home at 7,000ft. Nevertheless, the captain, Flg Off A. L. Wilson, and his comrades were frozen as they struggled to keep the 'Hally' airborne.

The radio was still working five minutes after the collision, but had to be switched off due to shorting; blue sparks were playing around the aircraft and there was risk of fire. In that short five minutes, before the radio was cut off, the operator was able to send out an SOS which was received in England. As a result Yorker was given special landing aids when it landed on an emergency airfield. The intercom was unserviceable as well as the airspeed indicator and DR compass, and many other vital instruments for flying and navigation. The 'Hally' dived 1,500ft after the collision with the pilot struggling to regain control. He managed to do this and brought the aircraft up to 11,000ft again. At this height it stalled,

but he managed to hold it at 7,000ft and at this height flew it home.

By this stage of the war two other marks of Halifax were in Bomber Command service alongside the B.III — the B.VI and B.VII. Both had a pressure transfer fuel system, additional fuel tankage and were 'tropicalised' to make them better suited for possible use in the Far East. The B.VI had four of the latest 1,675hp Hercules 100 engines which gave it a top speed of 290mph at 10,500ft. Service ceiling remained 20,000ft, the same as that of the B.III but the ranges and associated bomb loads were slightly increased: eg 2,160 miles with 7,000lb, or 1,260 miles with 13,000lb. The B.VII had Hercules XVIs — the power plant of the B.III — and came into being because airframe production exceeded the supply of Hercules 100s.

The last occasion when Bomber Command Halifaxes operated in force against the enemy was on 25 April 1945 when a heavy daylight attack was made on coastal gun batteries on Wangerooge island in the East Frisians. On 2/3 May Halifaxes of 100 (Bomber Support) Group flew diversionary radio countermeasures sorties (sometimes dropping bombs) against Flensburg, Schleswig-Holstein and elsewhere, in support of a main force attack on Kiel, Bomber Command's final raid of the war.

Bomber Command's Halifaxes flew 82,773 operational sorties during World War II, including 365 under Coastal Command control, and dropped 224, 207 tons of bombs and laid a large but unknown number of sea mines; 1,833 Halifaxes were reported missing.

The Avro Lancaster

During 1939 the Manchester was regarded as one of the most important bombers in the future night attack force in Bomber Command. But already the Vulture engine was giving anxiety because of teething problems and the eventual replacement of the Vulture engines by other types was under consideration. At the conference held at King Charles Street, Whitehall, on 12 December 1939 to discuss future bomber requirements, one of the decisions taken was to produce a new development of the Manchester. Projects for re-engining the Manchester with Napier Sabre or Bristol Centaurus engines in the 2,000hp class had already been undertaken, but the Sabre was urgently required for the Hawker Typhoon and the Centaurus was only in the early stage of development. With Rolls-Royce Merlin engines in mass production at several factories it was natural that the Avro design team should examine the possibility of installing four Merlins in the Manchester, this project initially being known as the Manchester III. This project used the basic fuselage, centre wing section and tail unit of the Manchester, with new outer wings increasing the span to 100ft. Four Merlins were installed in separate nacelles, two in the original Vulture position and the other two out on the new outer wings. The power of the four Merlins was well in excess of the power that would be available from two of the 2,000hp engines.

By the early summer of 1940 the project design of the new version of the Manchester was completed and the design was assessed by the Air Staff, who were enthusiastic about its potential. Given the Avro type number 683, the Manchester III was estimated to have a normal flying weight of 50,000lb, with normal overload at 55,000lb, and maximum overload of 57,000lb. At 57,000lb the new bomber was expected to carry 10,936lb of bombs for 1,500 miles. 8,000lb of bombs could be carried for 1,600 miles, and if the range was reduced to 1,000 miles then nearly 12,000lb of bombs could be carried, in each case at 245mph. At an economical speed of 190mph the Type 683 was expected to carry 8,000lb of bombs for 2,000 miles and 12,000lb for 1,350 miles. All these figures were a marked improvement over the Vulture-engined Manchester, and were generally similar to the Handley Page Halifax.

At that time it was considered by the technical departments of the Air Ministry and the RAF that the four-engined Manchester would be slightly inferior to the Halifax because it was a compromise, not designed from the outset to be powered by four Merlins. The Halifax had, of course, started life on paper as a twin-Hercules, and then twin-Vulture design, but had been re-drafted with four Merlins before structural engineering design had commenced, and thus could be considered to be a four-engined monoplane from an early stage in its design. The supremacy of the four-engined Avro design in later years showed what an excellent compromise the design proved to be.

The structural alteration to the basic Manchester airframe proved to be considerable and it was decided in November 1940 to name the new bomber Lancaster I, and put it into production after completion of current Manchester orders. A new specification, Lancaster 1/P.1, was written around the projected design, and this called for a cruising speed of not less than 250mph at 15,000ft. On weak mixture cruising power, with a 50min additional allowance at this power, the Type 683 was required to carry 7,500lb of bombs for not less than 2,000 miles. A maximum range without bombs of 3,000 miles was specified.

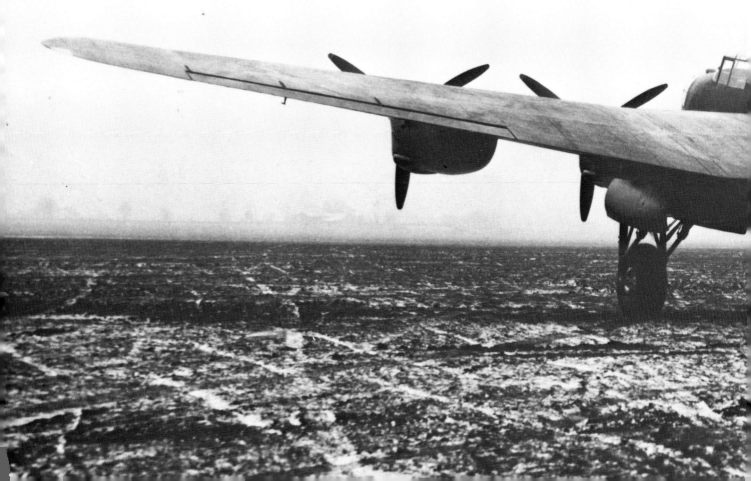

One of the features required from the design was the carriage of varied bomb loads and the following were specified: 1 × 4,000lb HC and 6 × 500lb GP bombs, 6 × 1,500lb 'A' mines, 6 × 1,900lb GP bombs and 3 × 250lb GPs, 6 × 2,000lb AP bombs and 3 × 250lb SAP bombs, 14 × 500lb GP bombs, 6 × 500lb AS bombs, 5 × 250lb AS bombs, 6 × 500lb AS bombs, 3 × 250lb AS bombs and 5 × 250lb SAP bombs, 6 × 1,000lb GPS and 3 × 250lb GPs, 14 × 500lb SAP bombs, 14 × 250lb GP, SAP, AS, LC or 'B' bombs, and 14 × 250lb small bomb containers. Later in its life, of course, the Lancaster was adapted to carry, in addition the 8,000lb HC bomb, 12,000lb HC bomb, 12,000lb Tallboy DP and 22,000lb Grand Slam DP bomb.

The first prototype Lancaster I was converted from a standard production Manchester, BT308, and it retained the small end fins and central fin of the twin-engined Avro bomber, although a new tail unit with twin fins and rudders was being designed for the new

bomber. Construction of the prototype was rapid and by the end of 1940 it was complete and being ground tested in preparation for its first flight, which took place on 9 January 1941. Flight trials proved to be very promising and it went to Boscombe Down in late February. The second prototype, DG595, also a converted Manchester, joined the test programme on 13 May and differed from the first in having the revised tail unit from the outset. Both prototypes continued to fly successfully during 1941, and in October, L7527, the first production Lancaster I, was completed. L7527 made its first flight, from Woodford, Cheshire, on 31 October 1941, and by the end of November four production

Above: A Lancaster of No 7 Squadron, Pathfinder Force, pictured over the sea with an escorting RAF Mustang.

The prototype Lancaster showing the original tail surfaces complete with central fin. / *IWM*

Lancasters had been completed. During November intensive flying trials were carried out at Boscombe Down, with L7527 and L7529, intended to highlight any problems before the new bomber entered service.

The name Lancaster evokes immediate thoughts of Bomber Command's supreme heavy bomber, flying night after night deep into Germany, delivering devastating blows or flying daring low-level missions against pin-point targets, but the early part of its career was marked by a number of problems, some of them serious. After six-hours of flying at Boscombe Down, L7527 was just taking-off when the starboard oleo rams became detached from the main undercarriage legs. It got airborne, but the pilot had to make a belly landing, doing damage to the underside. The second Lancaster at Boscombe Down, L7529, was grounded for a time while undercarriage modifications were carried out. L7530 was intended to replace L7527, but as this was required to be prepared for squadron use, L7535 was sent to Boscombe instead. L7529 recommenced flying and it was noticed that serious skin wrinkling was taking place on the wing upper surfaces, caused during excessive wing flexing.

As the intensive trials continued at Boscombe Down, 44 Squadron had been the unit selected to be the first to operate the Lancaster, its first three aircraft arriving on 24 December 1941. After a period of working-up the first operation by the squadron was on 3 March 1942, when four Lancasters laid mines and all returned to Waddington. Two Lancasters of the squadron carried out the first bombing sortie on 10 March. A second Lancaster squadron, 97, was fully equipped by mid-February 1942, and it flew its first operational sorties on 20 March. All the aircraft returned from this operation, but one crashed near Boston in circumstances that caused 5 Group to order all Lancasters to be grounded for inspection of the upper wing surfaces for traces of skin wrinkling. There was also anxiety about the wing tips and a modification was undertaken by Avro's to produce a revised tip.

In order to test the new tips under severe conditions, Lancaster R5539, at Boscombe Down, carried out a series of test dives and severe pull-outs as part of the intensive flying programme. On 18 April, it took off at midday to continue the test dive trials, at a weight of 60,000lb, and at about 1500hrs it was seen to emerge from cloud in a shallow dive at 4,000ft. It suddenly rolled 180 degrees to port, rolled level again and then dived into the ground at an angle of 60 degrees and exploded, making a crater 14ft deep. The aircraft was only carrying dummy bombs, but the explosion caused damage to houses some distance away. A significant piece of upper wing skin measuring 6ft x 3ft was found down the flight path outside the explosion area. The rear edge of the panel had been folded, clear evidence that the front row of rivets along the spar had pulled out and the panel had then folded back against the airflow. Five airmen were killed in the crash, which occurred at Charlton, near Hullavington, Wilts, including Wg Cdr P. S. Salter and Sqn Ldr J. D. Harris, experienced Lancaster pilots. At the time of the crash the Lancaster had made 80 steep dives during the course of its flying programme. As a result of this accident, a number of Lancasters were inspected along the front spar on the upper wing surfaces and all were found to have pulled rivets. Clearly this was a serious structural defect and urgent modifications to all Lancasters had to be made before operations could be resumed.

The intensive flying programme at Boscombe Down had totalled 110hr 55min and as a result of the crash of R5539 another Lancaster, L7529, flew a further 30hr to test the modified upper wing panelling and spar rivetting.

207 Squadron was the third to re-equip with the new Avro bomber, and eventually all the rest of the squadrons in 5 Group also received Lancasters during 1942. By March 1945 no fewer than 56 squadrons of Bomber Command were flying the Lancaster and it had shown itself to be the RAF's most successful heavy bomber of World War II.

The Lancaster B.1 had a wing span of 102ft and a length of 69ft

Above: Vic of Lancaster Is of No 207 Squadron pictured about June 1942. The nearest machine, R5570 EM-F, was eventually lost in a raid on Turin on the night of 8/9 December 1942.

Below: Crash-landed Lancaster of No 576 Squadron showing extensive signs of battle damage, the rear turret having broken off during the heavy landing. / IWM

Right: **Lancaster Variants.** (a) Lancaster B.Mk III (Special) converted for the Dams raid. (b) Lancaster with bulged bomb bay for 12,000lb HC bomb. (c) Proposal for a long-range bomber using special saddle tank. The prototype was flown but the system was not adopted. (d) Lancaster modified for carrying 12,000lb and 22,000lb deep penetration bombs. (e) Lancaster B.Mk VI with Rolls-Royce Merlin 85/87 engines in circular nacelles.

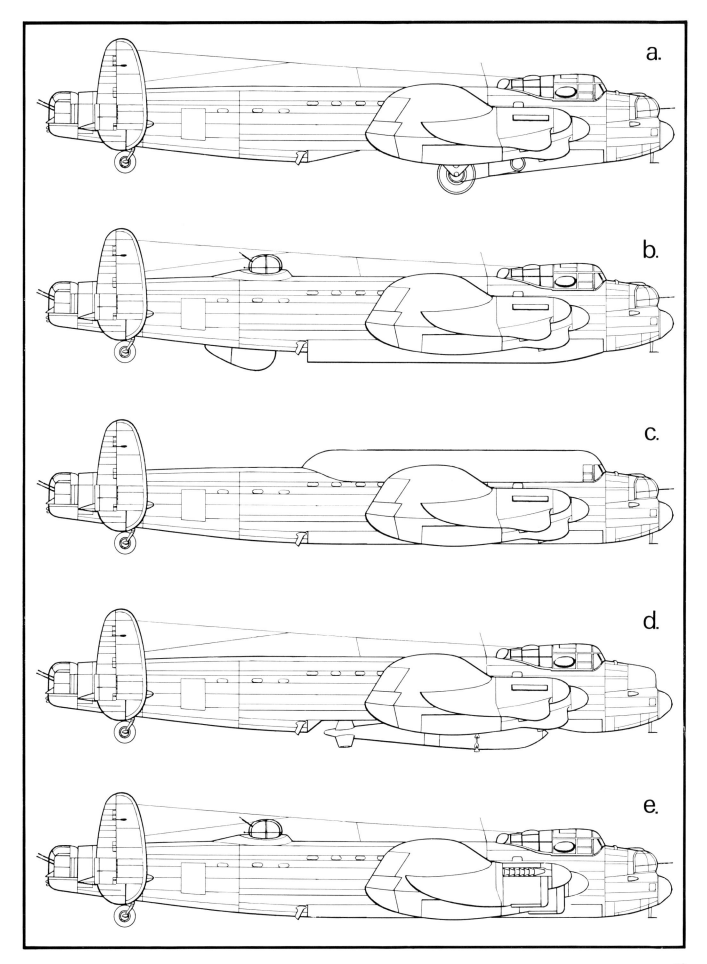

a.

b.

c.

d.

e.

79

6in (tail up). Normal loaded weight was 65,000lb, maximum bomb load 18,000lb, and defensive armament comprised ten .303in Browning guns, disposed two each in Frazer Nash nose, dorsal and ventral turrets, and four in a FN tail turret. The ventral turret was not, of course, installed when an *H2S* bulge was fitted, as was largely the case from 1943. Normal cruising of the B.1 at normal loaded weight was 160-170mph on the way to a target and 200mph after bomb release. Maximum speed at 15,000ft was 275mph in fully loaded condition and 287mph with light load. With a 7,000lb bomb load the Lancaster I could fly for 2,530 miles. A 12,000lb bomb load could be carried for 1,730 miles. Stalling speed at 50,000lb loaded weight was 92mph. Maximum diving speed was 360mph.

A special version of the B.1 had a strengthened bomb bay to take the 22,000lb Grand Slam deep penetration bomb, which it could carry for a range of 1,550 miles at 200mph at 15,000ft. Nose and dorsal turrets were removed and the Lancaster B.I (Special) had a maximum weight of 72,000lb; 33 Lancasters were converted into B.I (Specials). The total number of standard Lancaster B.Is built was 3,429, with two prototypes converted from Manchesters. Avro factories at Chadderton and Yeadon, Vickers-Armstrongs factories

at Chester and Castle Bromwich, Armstrong Whitworth at Baginton, Austin at Longbridge and Metrovick at Mosley Road, Manchester, all produced Lancasters. An order for 200 from Short and Harland at Belfast was not proceeded with.

So great was Lancaster production, coupled with the demands of Halifax, Spitfire, Mosquito, Hurricane, Barracuda, Welkin and Hornet production, that there was great danger of supply problems with Merlin engines. An alternative engine was therefore considered for the Avro bomber, the choice being the Bristol Hercules VI 14-cylinder air-cooled sleeve-valve radial engine. This was a natural alternative because it was in the same power class as the Merlin, and the only other engine of this power in mass production. The new Lancaster variant was designated the B.Mk II, and a prototype, DT810, was quickly assembled from standard production Lancaster parts and made its first flight on 26 November 1941. Production of the Lancaster II was undertaken by Armstrong Whitworth at Baginton in place of the Whitley, and the first Lancasters of this type, DS601 and DS602, were completed in September 1942. Trials squadron for introducing the type was No 61 at Syerston, Notts, which received its first Lancaster II in the middle of October 1942. The first Lancaster II operation was on the night of 11/12 January 1943. One of the major problems with the type soon became manifest: its average maximum height with full load was only 15,000ft, well below the normal Lancaster I cruising height and in a region where flak and

Above left: Fine study of a Hercules radial-engined Lancaster II secured from a Hampden whose tail can be seen in the foreground.

Below: An early production Lancaster I with its dorsal turret devoid of the fairing which came to be fitted on later aircraft.

Above right: Another study of the Lancaster II, this specimen being an aircraft of No 342 'Leaside' Squadron of the RCAF's No 6 Bomber Group which operated almost exclusively from Yorkshire. / *RCAF Official*

Below right: Bomb log of this veteran Lancaster B.X of No 419 'Moose' Squadron, RCAF, shows that it has completed 75 operational sorties. Several Lancasters did, in fact, considerably exceed the 100 sorties mark, leader being Mike Squared of Nos 103 and 576 Squadrons; it was a Mk III and bore the serial ED888. / *RCAF Official*

fighters were most active. On the credit side the Hercules engines, being air-cooled, were less vulnerable than the Merlins, with their additional glycol cooling equipment and radiators.

Turin, in northern Italy, was the target for several early Lancaster II raids and this entailed flying across the Alps — with some peaks as high as the maximum Lancaster II cruise height. The last raid of the war on Turin before the Italian surrender was on the night of 16 August 1943, when 14 of 115 Squadron's Lancaster IIs, each carrying a 4,000lb bomb and incendiaries, made the hazardous journey across the Alps, only one aircraft being lost.

Sir W. G. Armstrong Whitworth built 300 production Lancaster IIs at Baginton in addition to the Avro-assembled prototype, DT810, and these were issued to one flight of 61 Squadron and also Nos 115, 514, 409, 426, and 432 Squadrons. The type also served with several heavy conversion units and research establishments. It had a top speed of 265mph at 14,000ft and an economical cruising speed of 167mph at 15,000ft. Maximum range with small bomb load was 2,550 miles. Maximum bomb load was 14,000lb. The ventral turret was standard, as were enlarged bomb doors to facilitate the stowage of 8,000lb bombs.

As an insurance against supplies of home-built Rolls-Royce Merlin engines running into difficulties, either from demand to satisfy all the different types using the Merlin engine, or from temporary hold-ups in production caused by enemy bombing, the Packard company in America undertook mass production of the Rolls-Royce engine. In the natural sequence of events the American-built Merlins were available for installation in Lancasters and the first to have them installed was R5849, but a new mark number was allotted to a production version of the Avro bomber powered by Packard Merlin 28, 38 or 244 engines — Lancaster B.Mk III. The true prototype for the Mk III was W4114, but this new variant was virtually a Mk I re-engined with the American-built engines. Performance of the new version was generally similar to that of the standard B.Mk I. 2,990 Lancaster B.IIIs were built, which included 23 aircraft specially modified to carry the Wallis dam-busting bomb.

A similar version to the Mk III, also using Packard-built Merlins, was produced in Canada by Victory Aircraft Limited, a company formed by the National Steel Corporation of Canada under government control, to produce the Lancaster under the designation B.Mk X. 422 B.Xs were built and the majority were sent to Britain to equip the Canadian squadrons in 6 Group, Bomber Command. Armament was the same as that of the Mk I — including the two-gun ventral turret initially — and enlarged bomb doors to accommodate 8,000lb bombs were standard. One of the lesser-known variants of the Lancaster was the Mk VI, powered by four Merlin 85 or 87 engines in new nacelles with annular radiators and built to Specification B.14/43, calling, among other things, for a bomber capable of operating at heights of up to 35,000ft. Only a few Mk VI were produced (converted from Mk IIIs) and some were used by several squadrons of the Path Finder Force, chiefly 635 Squadron, for operational trials, sometimes acting as the Master Bomber's aircraft.

The final production version of the Lancaster was the B.Mk VII, basically a Mk I with two .5in guns in a Martin dorsal turret mounted nearer to the wing, and two .5in guns in the Frazer Nash rear turret. After VJ-Day the type became the B.Mk VII (FE) by virtue of tropicalised equipment originally intended for use by the Tiger Force in the Far East for the final campaign against Japan. Austin Motors built 180, but this mark was largely a postwar development.

Out of a compromise, expected at best to be slightly inferior to aircraft designed around four Merlin engines from the outset, the

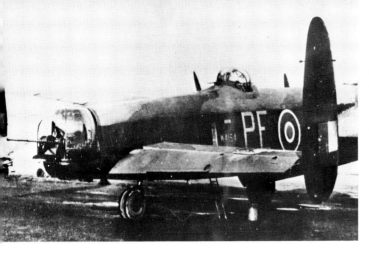

Lancaster became Bomber Command's most potent heavy bomber of World War II. But had it not been for the failure of the Vulture engine and its consequential effect of bringing about the demise of the Manchester, the mighty 'Lanc' might never have been evolved.

Ten VCs were won by Lancaster crew members, and stirring tales of how crippled 'Lancs' defied very heavy odds and safely returned home after having sustained serious battle damage abound in the squadron records. One such episode occurred when a Lancaster captained by Sqn Ldr H. F. Slade, an Australian commanding 156 (Path Finder Force) Squadron, was hit by flak before making its bombing run over Hamburg on 28/29 July 1944.

Slade released his bombs but the 'Lanc' then went into a slow

Above left: Annular air intakes in the engine cowlings distinguished the Lancaster B.VI from other models — except, of course, the larger Mk IV which was quickly renamed Lincoln. The B.VI was used in very limited numbers — less than ten in fact — and served with certain PFF units only.

Centre left: This Lancaster of No 635 Squadron of the Pathfinder Force is fitted with an Automatic Gun-Laying Turret (AGLT), known to Bomber Command as Village Inn and automatically sighted and fired at enemy aircraft. Only a few such turrets were in service when the war ended and they were introduced too late to make any difference to the air combat picture. */ IWM*

Below left: Away goes a Grand Slam from a Lancaster B.I (Special) of No 617 Squadron during a raid on the Arnsberg Bridge in March 1945. Only one other Lancaster squadron used the 22,000lb Grand Slam operationally in World War II — No 9 Squadron. */ IWM*

Above: Unusual tail turret on this Lancaster of No 1 Lancaster Finishing School is the Rose-Rice turret mounting two 0.50in guns. First turrets of this type went to No 150 Squadron which was re-formed to fly Lancasters on 1 November 1944, but they were relatively uncommon. */ via P. H. T. Green*

Below: In this air-to-air view of a Lancaster X the ventral turret is not fitted, but the deepened bomb doors are clearly seen. Note also the Martin mid-upper turret, a feature of late production aircraft of this mark.

spiral dive, out of control. Slade ordered his crew to prepare to bale out, but succeeded in getting the bomber back on an even keel. Helped by the navigator and the flight engineer he manhandled the Lancaster away from the target area and headed for home with only about 10 per cent aileron control. He had an anxious time while flying over the enemy coastal gun belt as he could not take evasive action without the danger of spinning out of control. He persevered, however, and by intelligent use of petrol only from the port tanks he established a better balance and less strenuous flying conditions. Once over the North Sea he headed for Woodbridge emergency airfield, and although his engines were undamaged he slowly lost height all the way. Any momentary loss of power or relaxation of his grim struggle with the controls would have sent the Lancaster crashing into the sea. When he reached the Suffolk airfield the 'Lanc' was down to 1,500ft and Slade called on his reserve of physical strength and mental tenacity to make a successful emergency landing from which his crew emerged safely, although the Lancaster was further damaged.

Another heroic story is that concerning an altogether amazing series of incidents which befell Flg Off J. H. Bryers, RNZAF, and his crew of a 61 Squadron Lancaster during a raid on Giessen one night in December 1944. First a fighter attacked them; then, just as the bombs were dropped, a nearby burst of flak sent their aircraft plunging out of control. A minute later incendiaries dropped from a bomber above hit the fuselage, followed almost immediately by a burst of fire from a fighter which killed the mid-upper gunner and set his turret alight. The blaze quickly gained a firm hold and a second fire developed in the port wing, sending long tongues of flame licking along the fuselage. Byers now ordered his crew to bale out but the wireless operator, busy over his set, did not hear the order. He remained aboard and, as the Lancaster flew on, managed to subdue the flames in the mid-upper turret. Byers, who had remained at the controls, thereupon decided to attempt an emergency landing on the Continent. Eluding a trailing fighter, he headed towards Liege on fixes supplied by his companion. In due course the 'Lanc' arrived over an airfield, and although it was unlighted and its short runway was normally only used by fighters, Byers managed a safe landing with the aid of the bomber's lights and Very cartridges.

Altogether, Lancasters of Bomber Command flew 156,192 operational sorties in World War II including 116 under Coastal Command control. They dropped 608,612 tons of bombs and laid a substantial number of sea mines; 3,345 Lancasters were reported missing.

The Boeing B-17 Fortress

Three marks of the American Boeing B-17 Fortress four-engined bomber were used by Bomber Command in World War II, but only the first of these was used in the type's primary role, the others being used for radio and radar counter-measures. The Fortress I, which did the bombing, was basically the USAAC B-17C version of the Flying Fortress, and the 20 examples supplied to the RAF were flown to Britain in the spring of 1941. Powered by four 1,200hp Wright Cyclone engines, they were armed with only one .303in nose gun and four .50in guns, two in ventral 'bathtub' and two in the beam positions, and their bomb load was a meagre 2,500lb. American Air Corps officers realised these particular Fortresses were already obsolete and urgently suggested to the RAF that they only be used for training crews, so that these crews might, later, know how to handle the improved B-17E Fortresses which were then in production and fly them into battle. The RAF authorities were also told that much practice was required to learn how to use the top secret Norden bomb sight and that the Fortresses were meant to fly in formation for their protection from fighter attacks.

These instructions were not followed, for the Fortresses, after undergoing modification, were issued to 90 Squadron in 2 Group and used mostly in twos and threes, beginning with a raid by three aircraft on Wilhelmshaven on 8 July 1941. The result was that these old, inadequately armed Fortresses proved far from successful in the high-altitude day bombing role, as recounted elsewhere in this volume. Problems included frozen guns, turbo-supercharger and engine failures at altitude, and vapour trails which latter gave the enemy a clear indication of the Fortresses whereabouts. Just 51 sorties were mounted by 90 Squadron in the period up to September 1941, when operations over Europe finally ceased, and no less than 25 of these had to be abandoned due, in the main, to one or more of the foregoing problems. Naturally, of course, none of this reached the British public, and it must have been with tongue very much in cheek that a Fortress I crew member gave the following account of a sortie against Emden in a radio broadcast:

'I have flown in the sub-stratosphere in a Fortress bomber over Holland, France, Norway and Germany. If the people on the ground in those countries have seen us at all, we have appeared no more than the tiniest dot in the sky. Their largest towns have seemed no bigger than a sardine tin laid flat on the perspex.

'On your first ascent, you are very much aware of flying in unexplored space, relying completely on oxygen, but after a few trips you become accustomed to new colours in the sky, and when from one point, only a hundred miles from the English coast, you can see right across Denmark into the Baltic, and into Germany by Hamburg, and the whole plain of Holland is spread out in front of you, you do little more than note it in your log. To us, who have carried out a good many attacks on the enemy, our Fortress seems no more difficult or less reliable than a good old Lysander at 1,000 feet. It's all a question of what you get used to.

'Before coming to our attack on Emden last week-end, I should

Another Fortress I which saw service with No 90 Squadron on high-altitude daylight raids.

like to give you two instances of why we have learned to have this trust in the Fortresses. I was in the Fortress which was attacked by seven fighters when we were returning from Brest. Three minutes after our bombs had gone the fire controller called out that there were seven enemy fighters coming up to us from the starboard quarter, 1,000 feet below. They closed in and there was almost no part of the Fortress which was not hit. Some of my friends in the crew were killed, others wounded. A petrol tank was punctured, bomb doors were thrown open, flaps were put out of action, tail tab shot away, tail wheel stuck half down, brakes not working, only one aileron any good and the rudder almost out of control. The centre of the fuselage had become a tangle of wires and broken cables, square feet of the wings had been shot away, and still the pilot managed to land the Fortress on a strange aerodrome. There is a testimony to the makers in America. Another time, when we were coming away from Oslo, part of the oxygen supply ceased and the pilot had to dive down swiftly through 19,000 feet. He pulled out and the Fortress landed safely at base. There is proof of the strength of the Fortress's construction.

'Fortunately these thrills are rare. Our attack on Emden last week-end was almost without incident, except, of course, for the dropping of the bombs by the Sperry sight with beautiful accuracy on the target. It was, in fact, a typical Fortress raid. We lost sight of the aerodrome at 3,000 feet, and never saw ground again until we were off the Dutch islands. Foamy white cloud, like the froth of a huge tankard of beer, stretched all over England and for about

thirty miles out to sea. The horizon turned — quite suddenly — from purple to green and from green to yellow. There was a haze over Germany, but I could see Emden 50 miles away. I called out to the pilot, in the sort of jargon we use in the air, "Stand by for bombing, bomb-sight in detent, George in, OK I've got her." Then the pilot says to me, "Let her go."

'The drill is that I push a lever on my left for the bomb doors to open, and on a dial in my cabin two arms move out like the hands of a clock to show us the position of the bomb doors. On and around the Sperry sight there are eleven knobs, two levers and two switches, to operate. On the bombing panel there are five switches and three levers to work and the automatic camera to start. I keep my eye down the sighting tube which, incidentally, contains twenty-six prisms, and with my wrist I work the release. As the cross hairs centred over a shining pin point in Emden on which the sun was glinting, the bombs went down. The pilot was told by means of an automatic light which flickered on as they dropped. We were still two miles away from Emden when we turned away. One of the gunners watched the burst. Almost a minute later he told us through the inter-com, "There you are, bursts in the centre of the something target," and back we came through those extraordinary tints of the sky.

'Over England there was a strange scene that I have noticed

before. The cloud formation exactly compared with the land below. Every bay and inlet was repeated in the strato-cumulus thousands of feet above, like a white canopy over the island. During the whole sortie I had only one thrilling moment. I saw a Messerschmitt coming towards us. He seemed an improved type, and I looked again. It was a mosquito which had got stuck on the perspex in the take-off and had frozen stiff. The windows usually are splashed with insect blood, but this fellow had seemed the right shape for a Hun. Otherwise, it was an uneventful, typical trip in a Fortress, with the temperature at minus 30 degrees below zero Centigrade.'

No 90's surviving Fortress Is were transferred to the Middle East or Coastal Command and not until the final months of the war did the Fortress re-enter Bomber Command's inventory, albeit in the shape of the vastly improved Mks II and III, counterparts of the USAAF's B-17F and G respectively. Two squadrons of 100 (Bomber Support) Group operated the Fortress II and III, although one of these previously flew Consolidated Liberators, and their task was to protect the main force heavies by jamming, with special equipment which they carried, the enemy's early warning radar, his AI radar and his fighter control VHF and HF radio communications.

Key factors which influenced the choice of the Fortress for this work were its capability of accommodating the necessary jamming devices, its relative invulnerability to fighters due to its high altitude performance (it could cruise at 28,000ft) and heavy armament (twin .50 guns in nose, dorsal turret, ventral turret and tail turret plus twin 0.50s in waist position, although none of these was necessarily installed).

The Fortresses for 100 Group were converted for their special role by Scottish Aviation Ltd at Prestwick. Their chin turrets were removed and replaced by *H2S* blisters, flame dampers were fitted to the exhausts, and racks of black boxes, the jamming devices, installed in their bomb bays. The operations of these Fortress jammers is outside the scope of this work, as indeed is that of the special Mosquitos, Lancasters, Stirlings, Halifaxes, Liberators etc. which also participated in the so-called 'War of the Ether', but their work has already been dealt with by Alfred Price in his excellent books *Instruments of Darkness* (William Kimber, 1967) and *Battle Over the Reich* (Ian Allan, 1973).

Right: A B-17C Fortress Mk I showing the ventral 'bath-tub' which was armed with a single 0.50in gun. / *British Official*

Below: A radio countermeasures Fortress III in all-black finish, carrying an H2S scanner beneath its nose. Just visible below the waist gun hatch on the port side of the mid-fuselage is a special chute for the dispensing of 'Window' or what is nowadays termed 'chaff'.

Plans for a Blenheim Replacement

Buckingham B.1 KV335 on test.

As related in Volume I, a conference was held in Whitehall on 12 December 1939, by members of various Air Ministry departments to discuss future plans for new bombers. One decision taken at that time was to develop a replacement for the Blenheim, a conventional light day bomber carrying a moderate bomb load over comparatively short range at fairly high speed, but also carrying good defensive armament. These requirements were embodied in Specification B.7/40, originally sent out to several companies, but eventually written specifically around a bomber variant of the Bristol Beaufighter. In the specification, the design was required to use as many components of the Beaufighter as possible to speed its entry into service, although as time progressed this became increasingly difficult.

Specification B.7/40 was for a light bomber to undertake short range bombing, often in direct support of ground forces, its duties to include high-level bombing and dive attacks. The aircraft was to carry a 4,000lb bomb load, including a single 4,000lb HC bomb, or a whole range of bomb types. It had to have a maximum speed of not less than 295mph at 5,000ft and a range of 900 miles when carrying a 1,000lb of bombs. Internal tankage was to provide a maximum range of 1,100 miles and additional tanks to give a ferry range of 2,000 miles without bomb load.

The B.7/40, like the Beaufighter, was to be powered by two Bristol Hercules engines. Some publications refer to the B.7/40 design as the Beaumont, but Air Staff and Air Ministry documents and minutes do not mention this name, referring colloquially to the project as the Beaubomber. Probably the title Beaumont was a suggested Bristol name put forward for adoption.

A critical analysis of the Bristol B.7/40 with the Douglas Boston III showed similarity in many respects, and in March 1941 changes were made to the design. In order to increase performance the two Hercules engines were discarded and the bomber was re-drafted around two Bristol Centaurus engines. The provision for dive bombing attacks was also removed from the specification. With Centaurus engines the maximum speed was expected to increase to 340mph at 8,000ft.

With the change to the bigger engines a new specification, B.2/41, was written around the design, which was still quoted in the document as being a bomber derivative of the Beaufighter. In fact, most of the Beaufighter components had by now been discarded and the B.2/41 was considered a new airframe throughout.

The specification called for a maximum speed of 370mph and a cruising speed of 300mph. Range with 2,000lb of bombs was to be 1,000 miles at 15,000ft and reinforcing range 2,000 miles. Two fixed .5in guns were in the nose, a mid-upper turret was to house four .303in guns and an under-mounting was to have two .303in guns. The B.2/41 was to be able to carry any of the following bomb loads: 1 × 4,000lb HC; 2 × 2,000lb HC or AP; 2 × 1,900lb GP; 2× 1,000lb GP; 6 × 500lb GP, SAP or AS; 6 × 250lb GP, SAP or LC; 6 × small bomb containers.

By 30 May 1941, the Bristol B.2/41 had been given the type name Buckingham and four prototypes had been ordered. At this time the Buckingham was considered to be one of the most important new types under development and was intended to replace the Blenheim on the Bristol production lines and in service to replace the Blenheim, Boston and Mitchell in the general light

tactical bomber role. The future unarmed, high-speed bomber for quick strikes against pin-point targets was to be Sydney Camm's B.11/41 and the de Havilland development of the Mosquito, both twin-Napier Sabre designs. The Buckingham was also expected to be developed in torpedo-bomber form to replace the Beaufort and Beaufighter.

Four hundred Buckinghams were on order by November 1941, under Specification Buckingham 1/P1, and a month later the number required rose to 800, with output expected to be 60 aircraft per month by 1944. Some changes were made to the specification requirements, including a maximum speed reduced to 355mph and cruising speed to 295mph.

Construction of the prototypes proceeded during 1942 under the Bristol type number 163. In its finalised form the Buckingham was a mid-wing monoplane powered by two Bristol Centaurus VII or XI eighteen-cylinder two-row radial engines, which were air-cooled by a fan rotating behind the four-bladed propeller, a development possibly inspired by the engine installation on the captured Fw190A. A crew of four was carried. The pilot was provided with four fixed .303in Browning guns mounted in the nose and a Bristol B.12 mid-upper turret housed four similar weapons. Two further guns of similar calibre were mounted in a ventral 'bathtub' firing under the tail. The bomb-aimer's position and optically-flat window were in the forward part of this ventral appendage. Twin fins and rudders were fitted to give a better field of fire for the rear gunners. The first prototype Buckingham was completed early in 1943 and on 4 February Cyril Uwins took the new day bomber into the air for the first time. The four prototypes were numbered DX249,

Below: The second prototype Bristol Buckingham seen fully equipped to production standard.

Above right: Bristol Buckingham twin-engined day bomber.

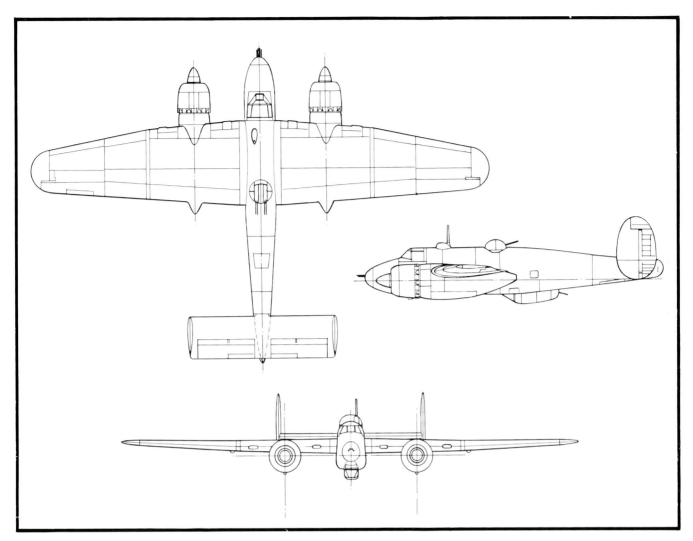

DX255, DX259 and DX266. The first two prototypes had vertical and horizontal tail surfaces of smaller area than on the third and fourth aircraft. Like the Beaufighter early in its career, the Buckingham had a marked tendency to swing on take-off and the larger vertical surfaces did not entirely cure the problem. The performance of the first prototype, DX249, was found during early tests to be similar to the estimates, but the inevitable increase in weight attendant on all aircraft under development and the increased drag of the enlarged tail surfaces reduced the top speed to 330mph, which was disappointing and little better than existing day bombers. At this time the Mosquito was beginning to realise its full potential as a very fast bomber able to penetrate enemy defences and deliver a 4,000lb bomb to a target over good ranges. Fears that it could be easily intercepted by the latest fighters proved to be unfounded, especially as installation of the two-stage Merlin 61 engines, which gave a good increase in performance, was found to be relatively easy. This enabled the Mosquito to keep one step ahead of opposing fighters in performance and the development of a pressure cabin permitted it to fly at increasing heights and thus lessen the chances of interception still more.

In the tactical role the Boston and Mitchell were proving to be excellent day bombers, but by 1943 they were being considered as due for replacement in the coming years.

Flight trials continued with the four Buckingham prototypes, and were augmented with production aircraft, commencing with KV301. Various problems arose during test flying, and while at Boscombe Down for evaluation Buckinghams were flown by various experienced bomber crews from 2 Group. Their reports

about the Buckingham were scathing: although the new bomber was intended to replace the Mitchell it was considered by the 2 Group officers to be inferior on many counts. The Mitchell was considered to be pleasanter to fly, more stable and better finished. The criticisms were particularly levelled at either the specification, which was said to be of 1936 vintage requirements, or to lack of consultation between designers and men with light bomber operational experience. The armament layout, particularly the four fixed .303in Browning guns in the nose, aimed by the pilot, was, in the opinion of the experienced light bomber crews, totally unsuitable. The Mitchell had power-operated .5in guns, whereas the Buckingham was armed with the much-less effective .303in Browning guns. The bomb aimer's position, in the small ventral bath, was inferior to the Mitchell nose, with its excellent all-round vision. The crews also objected to the marked tendency of the Buckingham to swing on take-off.

These criticisms from the very experienced 2 Group that was intended to operate the new bomber, came at a time when the future of the aircraft was already in doubt, due to the excellence of the Mosquito. There were also outstanding reports about Douglas's Boston replacement, the A-26 Invader, which could become available. In the meantime the Boston and Mitchell continued to do a fine job and had considerable operational life left. The Buckingham was thus abandoned as an operational bomber when the thirty-eighth production aircraft, KV337, had been built. It never entered service with a squadron, although its derivative, the Brigand, did equip squadrons in the postwar years, albeit not in Bomber Command.

The de Havilland Mosquito

By New Year's Day 1941 trials of the prototype Mosquito, W4050, were well under way at de Havilland's Hatfield facility and the company had been told by the Ministry of Aircraft Production's resident overseer that 150 more Mosquitos were to be ordered. Furthermore, additional manufacturing capacity was to be sought with a view to 'further extensive orders'.

W4050 reached 22,000ft, the expected cruising height, on 17 January but bad weather then grounded it for a while during which time the engine air intakes were modified to improve cooling and the nacelles lengthened, in two stages, to cure tailplane flutter caused by disturbed airflow. When official trials began at A & AEE Boscombe Down in late February, W4050's capabilities caused surprise, so the speeds were double checked. The results were confirmed as about 20mph faster than the Spitfire, but soon afterwards, on 24 February, W4050's fuselage fractured due to the tailwheel jamming while the aircraft was taxying across the muddy, bumpy airfield. The damage was soon repaired, however, and eventually, by 23 May, the A & AEE trials were complete, the

aircraft's excellent performance subsequently being confirmed by the RAE who stated that its maximum level speed was 392mph at 22,000ft at an all-up weight of 16,000lb, this speed being above estimates.

Meanwhile, on 11 January the company had been told that a reconnaissance prototype was to be built and that the balance of the original contract of March 1940 for 50 aircraft was to be completed as 19 reconnaissance and 28 fighter 'Mozzies', but no bombers. Later that winter, however, de Havilland were instructed to finish ten of them as bombers after all. By June, W4050 had been joined on trials by the other two prototypes, W4052 (fighter) and finally W4051 (PR), and in that same month de Havilland's were told to build Mosquitos in large quantities both in Britain and Canada.

Mosquito bombers became operational in the early part of 1942, first production model being the B. Mk IV which existed in two main versions: The Series I or PRU/Bomber Conversion Type, of which nine were built (W4064-72); and the Series II of which 50

In this view the Mk XVI's characteristic bulged bomb bay is seen to advantage.

were built (in three non-consecutive blocks between DK 284 and 339, one of which, DK 324, was converted into a PR.VIII on the production line).

Selected to receive the Mosquito first was 105 Squadron of 2 Group, which had previously flown Blenheims. Deliveries to the unit began on 15 November 1941, with W4064, and by the end of May 1942, when the 'Thousand Bomber' raid on Cologne took place, it had eight on strength and was ready to begin operations. The first sorties came only a matter of hours after the big raid ended. Four 'Mozzies' were despatched from Horsham St Faith to stoke up Cologne's fires with 500 and 250lb bombs. The city was obscured by thick smoke and clouds so the bombs were dropped by dead reckoning. One Mosquito failed to return.

During the ensuing months 105 Squadron gradually developed two distinct types of low level tactics, the really low level and the shallow dive, both types often being employed together on the same target. The low level attack was delivered by a single 'Mozzie' or a small formation which approached the target from the lowest possible level and released their bombs as they flew across it. The shallow dive attack was made by a second formation which climbed rapidly to about 2,000ft just before the target area was reached and then peeled off and dived straight down on to the target, releasing their bombs at about 1,500ft. The 'Mozzie's' bomb load, by the way, was doubled from its original 1,000lb before it entered service. De Havilland engineers did this by cropping the bomb vanes, thus making possible the stowage of four 500-pounders instead of four 250-pounders. Eventually, as we shall see, it was doubled again.

On 19 September six Mosquitos attempted a high level daylight raid on Berlin, the first of the war; only two reached the target area and they found it covered in cloud. Only one aircraft probably did manage to bomb Berlin, and that was DK337 N-Nuts which dropped its load on dead reckoning. Enemy fighters were active and one Mosquito was shot down; a second 'Mozzie' was damaged and jettisoned its bombs near Hamburg. Six days later four Mosquitoes, using Leuchars as a forward base, set out to make a low level precision attack on the Gestapo HQ in Oslo. Three Fw190s intercepted them as they attacked in pairs, and one 'Mozzie' was seriously damaged and forced to crash in Sweden. However, the other bombers delivered a pinpoint attack on the target and one of the Fw190s is known to have crashed, either being forced out of control by a 'Mozzie's' slipstream or affected by bomb blast.

The Mosquitos had expected 10/10th cloud at 2,000ft over Oslo, and no fighters; but instead they found a cloudless sky, and Fw190s. The enemy fighters pursued the three survivors but were unable to catch them. However, this and similar incidents on other occasions showed that the 'Mozzie's' speed margin was slight and various schemes were tried to improve it. Polishing the aircraft was one of these ideas, but in the end the best solution proved to be the replacement of the normal shrouded saxophone flame-damping exhausts with unshrouded oval-ended stubs, although the shrouded exhausts were kept for night operations. Remotely controlled rearward-firing scare guns were suggested for the nacelles (as they had been, in fact, during the 'Mossie's' design stage) but although a trial installation was effected by Rose Brothers and ground tested at Scampton the idea was abandoned.

By the end of November 1942, 105 Squadron had flown 282 operations sorties with Mosquitos, nine-tenths of them in broad daylight, and had dropped 330 tons of bombs; 24 aircraft had been lost, a loss rate of approximately eight per cent, whereas Bomber Command's night bomber losses were currently about five per cent.

During the following month a second Mosquito bomber squadron, No 139, began to operate alongside No 105, and before long they were both ranging far and wide over North-West Europe and frequently making front-page news with their daring low level precision attacks on pin-point targets. Centres 'stung' by the Mosquitos included Copenhagen (diesel workshops), Le Mans (Renault aero-engine factory), Liège (armaments works), and Paderborn and Nantes (railway maintenance facilities). A particularly outstanding raid was that of 3 March by 139 Squadron on the molybdenum washing plant at Knaben in Norway at almost full squadron strength. Molybdenum is a metallic element used in the production of high-speed steels and as the target supplied four-fifths of Germany's molybdenum it was rated high in importance. Sqn Ldr Bagguley, A Flight commander, was detailed to lead his formation in a low level assault, and was to be followed by the shallow-divers led by the CO, Wg Cdr Peter Shand. They made for Flamborough Head, then flew low over the North Sea before crossing the clear snow-clad Norwegian mountains among which the target lay. Smoke from the low level attack usefully marked the target for the shallow divers and not a single bomb was wasted, as photographs later confirmed. One Mosquito failed to return from the raid (shot down by Fw190s) and another was badly hit but crash-landed safely.

The character of 105 and 139 Squadrons' missions began to change in the latter part of April 1943: daylight and dusk raids at low level began to give way to night raiding at heights of over 20,000ft. One of these raids was against Berlin on 20/21st, the first high level nuisance raid made on the German capital. Eleven

'Mozzies' were involved and the raid was made to divert the enemy's attention from a large force of heavies which was attackng Rostock and Stettin that same night. The 'Mozzies' bombed Berlin from 16,000 to 23,000ft, in moonlight and clear weather, and afterwards maintained height until the enemy coast had been crossed. Enemy fighters were active and one managed to shoot down over the Zuider Zee the Mosquito flown by No 139's CO, Wg Cdr Peter Shand, who had led many notable 'Mozzie' raids.

On 27 May came the last low level dusk raid which Nos 105 and 139 Squadrons made and, fittingly, it was the most ambitious op yet attempted by low-flying 'Mozzies'. There were two targets; the Schott and Genossen optical glassworks, and the Zeiss optical instrument factory, both in the little town of Jena, 300 miles inside Germany, about 45 miles south-west of Leipzig. Wg Cdr R. W. Reynolds, who had succeeded Wg Cdr Shand as CO of 139 Squadron, led the raid in DZ601 B-Beer, with Flt Lt Sismore as his navigator, and it was extremely successful. Here is Sismore's first-hand account as recorded in the squadron's archives:

'On the morning of 27 May I was called to the operations room and shown the targets for the day — the Schott Glass Works and Zeiss Optical Instrument Works, both at Jena, 45 miles from Leipzig. This looked far more interesting than our more usual railway targets, and I then realised why we had recently concentrated so

Below: A Mosquito B.IX fitted with 50-gallon drop tanks.

much on low level flying training. A trip like this had to be good, and I, for one, was thankful for this training before the day was out. The trip involved our deepest penetration into Germany, but as our longer trips were usually the most successful, everyone was quite pleased. The route was, as usual, very carefully chosen, with regard to flak defences, fighter areas, and difficulties of low level navigation. An attempt was also made to fool the German Observer Corps as to the target and so maintain the element of surprise and prevent accurate fighter interception. The raid was to be led by Wing Commander Reynolds and myself.

Briefing began quite early, as it is a fairly lengthy business, especially when a long trip is involved. We were lucky in having some very good photographs and sketches of the targets and target area, and with the help of the epidiascope we were able to get a good idea of the approach to the target and the bombing run. The detailed plan of attack was carefully explained by the group captain until everyone was certain of his own part, from the time of take-off to the planned getaway and return home. The met officer talked about the weather, and it seemed almost perfect, low cloud and poor visibility in the fighter danger area, giving cover, clearing at the target to give a good opportunity for an accurate run on. Unfortunately the weather still has a habit of doing the wrong thing at the last moment.

Briefing over, we went back to the crew room, collected parachutes, etc, walked over to the waiting aircraft, climbed aboard and began to settle ourselves as comfortably as possible. Very soon all engines were started and we slowly taxied to take-off position. All aircraft took off in quick succession and we had a few minutes to get into formation before the time came to set course.

With everyone comfortably in position we set off, low over the aerodrome and heading for the Dutch coast. Weather was clear, sunny, and rather warm, and as we crossed the sandy beaches of our own coast the sea looked very cool and inviting.The sea crossing was fairly short and soon we began to increase speed. The flat coast of Holland appeared ahead, first as a grey line on the horizon, quickly becoming clearer, until we could see the beach and sea wall. Right ahead of us, just on the coast, were three wireless masts about a mile apart. It was impossible to turn the formation round them and we flew between two of them, hoping that there were no connecting wires — we were lucky! One gun began firing here but seemed to be ineffective. In a few minutes we came to the Zuider Zee, to find a fleet of small fishing boats ahead, some two hundred altogether, and I think the fishermen were rather surprised as the formation opened out a little and passed low between their masts.

The Zuider Zee seemed almost as wide as the North Sea, but eventually we reached the reclaimed and deserted Polder, and then the old coastline of Holland. The weather was still clear, and the little red villages of Holland looked very quiet and peaceful. We crossed the German frontier and the River Ems, and turned south, still flying low over undulating, well-wooded country. Visibility was very good and I could clearly see the spires and chimneys of Münster, some 12 miles away to the west. We could tell by now that something was wrong with our weather forecast, for the expected cloud had not yet appeared.

As we got down to the east of the Ruhr industrial area the country became hilly and more interesting, and now the cloud slowly began to build up ahead of us, in the area where we had hoped it would break. We flew between the Möhne and Eder Dams which had recently been breached, and we got accurate flak from another smaller dam in this area. Soon after this two aircraft had the misfortune to collide, and both went down into the hillside. It looked a nasty mess.

As we crossed the River Weser south of Kassel we could see

evidence of damage caused by the flood of water from the Eder Dam. The hilltops gradually got higher and higher, until we were flying in quite mountainous country, and although we kept as far as possible in the valleys we had to cross some of the lower peaks, and we were quite high above the deeper valleys. One house was built on the top of a small coneshaped hill, and as we flew past in the valley the door opened and a man walked out. I don't think he'll ever be more surprised at seeing Mosquitos speeding by, the nearest one level with him and some 200 yards away! On top of another hill was an observer post, its occupant scrutinising us through binoculars. No doubt he was soon passing on the gen by telephone.

The weather conditions were steadily deteriorating. The cloud was on the hilltops, and as we crossed them we had to switch lights on to keep the formation together, and there was quite a danger of running into one of the higher peaks. In the valleys it was a little better, although mist was quite thick and visibility less than a mile. We began to think that weather conditions would make the attack impossible, but as we reached our last turning-point before the target we were able to get into the valley of the River Saale, which would take us to the target. By this means we could keep clear of the cloud, although the visibility was now down to a thousand yards.

We came to the autobahn three miles south of the town and began the bombing run, peering into the gloom for the target. Just as it appeared out of the mist I saw the balloons and gave a startled shout — Wing Commander Reynolds picked his part of the target and we bombed the Schott Works from just above the tops of the tall chimneys. Just as the bombs were released flak hit the port airscrew and side of the fuselage a frightening bang, then some smoke and fumes entered the cockpit. Tracer was pouring up and we were still in the balloon barrage. The wing commander was taking violent evasive action and making a get-away along the valley to the north-west. I was talking on the inter-com trying to

help him to avoid the balloons, and it was not until we were clear that I realised that the inter-com wires had been severed and all my talk had been wasted. Once clear of the balloons we climbed into cloud and I realised that the wing commander was wounded. I got out first aid kit and made a rough bandage, which helped to stop the bleeding. He said it was numbed and didn't hurt too much.

We flew in cloud for some time, until it began to break, then we had to come down again to low level for safety. By this time it was getting dark and I had great difficulty in seeing enough of the ground detail to map-read. We flew over one well-defended town where the gunners seemed to take a great dislike to us, putting up a heavy concentration of light flak, but we were lucky enough to escape further damage. Eventually we were back over Holland again, and towards the mouth of the Rhine flew over a large flooded area, due, I think, to the released waters of the Möhne Dam. We reached the coast with just enough light to see the beach, a quiet spot, undefended, and then set course for base. Over the sea I went into the nose to check the bomb gear, and found that a piece of the port airscrew had been forced through the side of the fuselage and had smashed a lot of the equipment, luckily a fraction of a second after the bombs had left the racks.

We were soon across the North Sea and over England, and then up came the friendly lights of the flarepath, and in a few minutes we were back on the ground again.

After the doctor had decided that the wing commander's wounds were not too serious we went up to interrogation, and as the others came in pieced together the whole story of the raid.

Below: Line-up of Mosquito B.IVs of 105 Squadron at RAF Marham, Norfolk, in December 1942 when the squadron was operating as part of 2 Group, Bomber Command. / *Aeroplane*

Above right: de Havilland Mosquito B.Mk XVI.

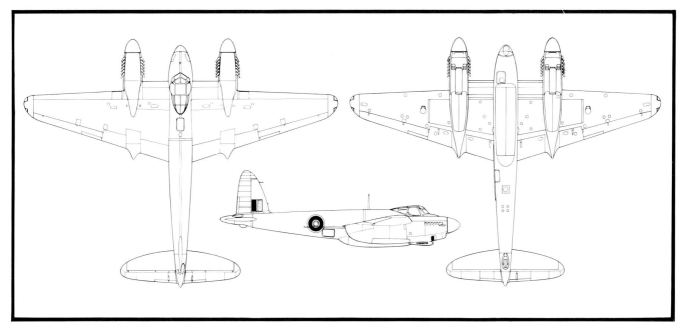

Finally we got away to the mess for a meal, but just before going to bed we saw again how luck had been with us — another piece of flak had torn wing commander Reynold's battledress two inches from his neck, another two inches and . . . But that is another story — the wing commander now has a new battledress.'

On 1 June 1943 2 Group became part of the newly formed 2nd Tactical Air Force under the temporary control of Fighter Command pending the formation of the Allied Expeditionary Air Force for the invasion of Europe. However, 105 and 139 Squadrons were retained by Bomber Command and now became part of 8 Group, the Path Finder Force, which was commanded by AVM D. C. T. Bennett. This group already had a Mosquito bomber unit on strength, 109 Squadron, which had received its first nine Mk IVs in July and August 1942 for trials of the new *Oboe* radar bombing aid, which used two ground stations and enabled an aircraft to follow a radar beam to its target and to achieve considerable accuracy in locating it blind. It was effective up to approximately the Ruhr. It could only be used by a few aircraft at one time and the range was proportionate to the bomber's altitude. It was thus an excellent aid to target marking by PFF Mosquitos which could reach much greater heights than the heavy Lancasters and, when coupled with the use of the ingenious new target indicator bombs that were developed, it revolutionised bombing accuracy. The first *Oboe* ground stations were erected on the East Coast in 1942 and on the night of 20/21 December six of 109 Squadron's *Oboe* Mosquitos began their operational career by a calibration raid against a power station at Lütterade in Holland. Other experimental raids followed in January and February 1943, and by the opening of March the *Oboe* Pathfinders were ready to lead a major attack, which came, as recounted elsewhere in this volume, on 5/6 March when Essen suffered the opening blow of the Battle of the Ruhr.

When 105 Squadron was transferred to 8 Group it became the second *Oboe* marker unit, and thereafter, with 109 Squadron, it made a major contribution to the overall success of the bomber offensive. Both these squadrons received the high-flying Mosquito B.IX in 1943, as did also 139 Squadron whose role was night high level nuisance bombing. This mark had 1,680hp two-stage Merlin 72/73 or 76/77 engines, and first flew in March 1943, a converted B.IV (DZ540) serving as the prototype. The Mk IX had an operational ceiling of about 31,000ft outward bound and 36,000ft

homeward bound, and in addition to the internal bomb load it could carry two 500 pounders under the wings. The advent of the Mk IX was timely, for by the autumn of 1943, 139 Squadron's B.IVs were making nuisance raids over the Ruhr flying at around 27-28,000ft and were being damaged on about half of their sorties, albeit in most cases only superficially. For the record, 8 Group's first operational Mosquito B.IX sorties were flown by 1409 Flight on 21 June 1943, when four aircraft attacked Krefeld.

Meanwhile, in May 1943, work had begun at Hatfield, by de Havilland's, on adapting the Mosquito to accommodate a 4,000lb 'cookie', in each of three versions: general purpose (GP), medium case (MC) and high explosive (HE). Initial test installation was effected on Mosquito IV DZ594 and entailed suspending the bomb from a single hook on a bridge of two spruce beams attached to the front and rear spars of the wing; enlarged, swollen bomb doors were fitted, aft of which was a small fairing to help smooth out the air flow. DZ594 first flew in July and later that month it was sent to the A & AEE at Boscombe Down for tests carrying the bomb, because its all-up weight of some 21,500lb did not permit it to be safely taken off from the airfield at Hatfield. The aircraft was returned to Hatfield in August for minor modifications necessitated by a sticking bomb-loading winch, but when this had been cured stability problems arose during flight testing, and pending the cure of this new problem the A & AEE provisionally passed the modified Mk IV for service with large elevator horn balance, rear camera removed and ballast added in the nose. Some modified B.IVs — B.IV (Specials) as they were known, were allotted to the PFF's newly-formed Light Night Striking Force early in 1944 and on 23/24 February DZ534, DZ637 and DZ647 of 627 Squadron, from Oakington, became the first 'Mozzies' to drop 'cookies' operationally, during a raid on Düsseldorf.

The 4,000lb bomb modification had also been authorised for the Mosquito Mk IX, but in service the stability problems were never fully overcome on either it or the Mk IV (Special) and thus few Mk IVs or IXs were ever modified. However, the next and final major stage in 'Mozzie' bomber development, the 'cookie'-carrying B.XVI proved highly successful and became the LNSF's mainstay. The prototype, MP469, flew in November 1943 and, thanks to its pressure cabin and Marshall blower which permitted full exploitation of its Merlin 72 engines, had an operational ceiling of 35,000ft. It came on the scene only just in time, for by December 1943, when production deliveries began, the Germans had developed special anti-Mosquito flak which was very accurate to around 40,000ft, twice the height at which the four-engined heavies usually bombed from. It was particularly dense around Berlin, and often moved up and down in a deadly carpet to deal with raiders flying at all heights. The 'Mozzie' B.XVI's ceiling, while still short of the maximum ceiling of this flak, was naturally welcomed by the LNSF's crews, who, by the way, underwent training in decompression chambers to ensure that they were not subject to aeroembolism or 'bends'.

No 139 Squadron was the first to operate the B.XVI — but not to drop a 'cookie' — when, on 10/11 February 1944, ML940 O-Orange visited Berlin. This squadron's 'Mozzies', whose job was to lead the LNSF, were by this time a mixture of IVs, IXs, XVIs and Canadian-built MkXXs. Some of them already carried *G-H*, a radar device in which the *Gee* navaid was combined with the *H*-system; the latter worked like *Oboe* in reverse, position plotting being done in the aircraft. Eventually about half of 139's 'Mozzies' had this aid, which had no range limitations although it was not as accurate as other navaids. The rest of the aircraft came to be equipped with *H2S* and, like similarly-equipped heavies, were officially known as 'Y' aircraft. Getting back specifically to the Mosquito B.XVI, the first examples to drop 4,000lb bombs on the enemy were 139 Squadron's ML941 N-Nuts and ML942 F-Freddy on 2/3 March 1944, when the target was München Gladbach. Thereafter a steady flow of B.XVIs reached the LNSF (or Fast Night Striking Force, as it became known) and it was the hope of AVM Bennett that a fleet of 200 would become available, but in the event many were completed, instead, as PR aircraft. However, six of his squadrons received B.XVIs before VE-Day, although only four, Nos 128, 571, 608 and 692, were fully equipped during that time.

As already mentioned, Mosquitos were also built in Canada. Production was centred at de Havilland Canada's Downsview factory, outside Toronto, numerous outside contractors being involved, of course, making everything from fuselages and wings to flaps and windscreens. First Canadian variant was based on the B.IV Srs II and powered by a Packard Merlin 31 engine; it was known as the B.VII originally but later became the B.XX (with Packard Merlin 31s or 33s). Some fighter-bomber and dual control trainer Mosquitos were also built at Downsview, but there was also a further straight bomber model, the B.25 with Packard Merlin 225s and a 2,000lb bomb load. A total of 135 B.XXs and 343 B.25s were delivered to Britain between August 1943 and mid-1945 (70 Mk 25s subsequently being handed to the Navy and four converted to carry 4,000lb bombs) and these types were used by three squadrons in 8 Group, Nos 139, 608 and 627, plus No 1655 Mosquito Training Unit.

Something has already been said about 139 Squadron's part in 8 Group's nuisance bombing offensive, but mention can now be made of the fact that one of this squadron's many notable achievements was the inauguration of Operation Ploughman, in which aircraft made 'Siren Tours', bombing several targets on one sortie. Between 20/21 February and 27/28 March 1945, it led each of 36 consecutive night attacks which Mosquitos of the Fast Night Striking Force made on Berlin. Bomber Command's heavies did not attack the German capital in 1945 but from the beginning of the year until the Russians captured it no fewer than 3,900 Mosquito bomber sorties were despatched to the 'Big City'. They dropped more than 4,400 tons of bombs on it, including 1,479 four-thousand pounders. Only 14 'Mozzies' failed to return from these operations, which represented about half their independent contribution to the offensive in 1945. It is of interest to note that the Berlin round trip of 1,200 miles took a Mosquito about four hours.

From March 1944, *Oboe* Mosquitos of 105 and 109 Squadrons

were often used on daylight operations. They led the heavies which neutralised the railway network of France and the Low Countries prior to the invasion of Normandy, and afterwards they led them in attacking enemy troop concentrations near Caen and V-1 sites in the Pas de Calais. On 27 August they made their first daylight trip to Germany when they marked the oil plant at Homberg in the Ruhr for some 200 Halifaxes of 4 Group.

On the night of 12/13 May 8 Group Mosquitos flew their first minelaying mission when a tiny force was sent to block the Kiel canal. After reaching Heligoland at a height of 10,000ft, the 'Mozzies', three Mk XVIs and ten Mk IVs of 692 Squadron from Graveley, in Huntingdonshire, turned south-eastwards in a shallow dive, and then due east for the last 14 miles run-up to the target in a steeper dive down to 300 feet. One Mosquito was shot down and all except one of the remainder successfully dropped their mines in the canal, which was closed for seven days after this operation. It was then partially re-opened, but owing to shipping losses was quickly closed again for another three days.

On the very eve of D-Day, Mosquitos of 105 and 109 Squadrons marked for the main force heavies ten gun emplacements on the Normandy coast. No 8 Group's 'Mozzies' remained active right up

Below: A 4,000lb 'Cookie' high-capacity bomb is hoisted into the bomb bay of a Mosquito B.IV Srs II of 692 Squadron, Fast Night Striking Force, at RAF Graveley, Huntingdonshire, in the spring of 1944.

Above right: Ready for off. A Mosquito B.XVI of 128 Squadron, Fast Night Striking Force, prepares to leave its base at RAF Wyton, Hunts, on a mission against Berlin on 21 March 1945.

to the end of hostilities, and during the final months 105 and 109 Squadrons often shared with No 139 the job of leading the entire Mosquito force in night raids. On 8/9 April the advent of an improved type of *Oboe* enabled 105 and 109 Squadrons to visit Berlin for the first time since joining the PFF, and thereafter they hit it many more times up to 20/21 April, when bombing of the Big City ended. For the record, Mosquito B.XVI MM929, piloted by Flg Off A. E. Austin, was the last RAF aircraft to bomb Berlin, at about 2.14am on 21 April. The final bombing sorties by 8 Group 'Mozzies' were flown on 2/3 May when the targets were the town of Kiel and the airfields at Husum and Eggebeck.

In all, 8 Group's Mosquito target-markers and Fast Night Strikers flew 26,255 operational sorties during the war at a cost of 108 aircraft missing plus 88 written off as a result of battle damage. (Figures for all Mosquito bombers operating in Bomber Command, ie those of 2, 5 and 8 Groups, were 28,639 bombing sorties and 110 sea-mining sorties flown, at a cost of 171 aircraft missing and 114 destroyed or damaged, 23 of them due to enemy action.) Total load dropped by 8 Group's 'Mozzies' alone is known to have included some 10,000 'cookies', or 26,000 tons of high explosive, a remarkable achievement for a little, unarmed, wooden, two-man aircraft, which flew 68 per cent of its missions when heavy bombers were not operating. The group's Mosquitos attacked Berlin on no less than 170 occasions between August 1943 and April 1945, sorties varying from less than six per night until a climax was reached on 21/22 March 1945, with a total of 139. In the final months of the campaign their losses were down to one per 2,000 sorties, a Bomber Command record.

One of 8 Group's 'Mozzie' squadrons, No 627, was attached to 5 (Lancaster) Group from April 1944 and largely took over the low-level dive-marking role pioneered by Leonard Cheshire VC in the few 'Mozzie' FBVIs operated by 617 Squadron of dam-busting fame. In Cheshire's case this involved diving towards the aiming point at an angle of about thirty degrees and from a height of a thousand feet or less often much less, to release red spot fire target markers by visual aim, using the gunsight. The initial marking could then be backed up by more red spot fires dropped by Lancasters from higher altitudes and then bombed from still higher level by the main force. Meanwhile, the whole operation could be controlled and directed by radio telephone from the 'Mozzie' still flying low enough to observe the aiming point clearly. Cheshire first tested this daring and ambitious dive marking technique operationally on the night of 5/6 April 1944, against an aircraft factory at Toulouse. Two Lancasters of 617 Squadron acted as backers-up, dropping red spot fires and one 8,000lb bomb apiece, and the factory was then bombed 'with tremendous effect' by about 140 Lancasters of 5 Group. Daylight reconnaissance photographs later showed that nearly all the buildings in the target area had been demolished or heavily damaged.

Unassisted by mechanical aids, 627 did for 5 Group what 8 Group's *Oboe* 'Mozzies' did for much of Bomber Command, but whereas they relied on height and speed for safety, 627 utilised the 'Mossie's' manoeuvrability and high speed at low levels. Normally they dived from 3,000ft to 1,000ft to mark their targets, and a mission which sums up their skill and daring was the raid on the Usine Lictard at Tours in May 1944. A few days previously this small factory had been the target for a high altitude raid by the USAAF and remained untouched. No 627's Mosquitos marked it with ease, the only hold up occurring when the first markers fell straight *through* the glass roof of the factory and almost disappeared from view!

From April 1944, No 627 operated from Woodhall Spa, having previously operated from Oakington, and it was while flying in a Mosquito XX of this squadron on 19/20 September 1944 that Wg Cdr Guy Gibson VC met his death. The dam-busting hero had volunteered to act as master bomber in a raid on Rheydt near the Ruhr as a change from an irksome desk job and his 'Mozzie' crashed in Holland on the way home, killing both himself and his navigator. Both men were subsequently buried in an unnumbered communal grave seven miles from Bergen-op-Zoom.

No 2 Group's American Light Bombers:
Boston, Ventura and Mitchell

Although 1941 saw the emphasis shift increasingly towards a night strategical bomber offensive carried out by medium and heavy bombers, a campaign which became synonymous in public minds with Bomber Command, one entire group of the Command, 2 Group, was then still equipped with Blenheim IV light bombers. In April 1941 the Expansion and Re-equipment Policy Committee agreed that ultimately the light bomber squadrons should be reduced to a minimum, but due to a forthcoming supply of American aircraft, some of which had been ordered by the British Purchasing Commission in 1940, this was not immediately possible and current crew training schedules would provide a surplus which could only be absorbed by forming light-bomber squadrons.

The Blenheims were employed on daylight operations against Germany and the occupied countries, both independently and in conjunction with Fighter Command during the summer of 1941. Targets included enemy shipping north of the Straits of Dover, power stations, shipbuilding yards, locomotives, steelworks and railway marshalling yards. On 12 August deep penetration of Germany was attempted, 54 Blenheims, with strong fighter escort as far as the Dutch coast, being sent to bomb, from low level, two power stations near Cologne, but this experiment was not repeated, and even in France penetration was not attempted farther than the Lille region, the offensive being almost purely tactical and against fringe targets. Some Blenheim squadrons were detached to the Mediterranean during 1941 and achieved commendable results in an anti-shipping role from Malta, albeit at a high cost. Meanwhile, the Blenheims of 2 Group remained 20 per cent of Bomber Command's numerical strength, though not, of course, of its striking power, although they, and indeed their American successors, always seemed to be a misfit to Bomber Command's 'top brass' after the main strategic night bombing offensive had begun to get under way.

First of the American light bombers (they were classified as medium bombers in their early days but had become light bombers by the time they entered RAF service) to operate with 2 Group was the Douglas DB 7B Boston III. With longer range, but otherwise similar both in appearance and performance to the DB-7A which had been ordered by the French just before the collapse in 1940, the Boston III was a twin 1,600hp Wright Double Cyclone-engined, tricycle-undercarriaged 3-seat day bomber with a maximum speed of 304mph at 13,000ft, a range of 1,020 miles with full bomb load of 2,000lb, and a service ceiling of 24,250ft. Defensive armament comprised four fixed .303in Browning guns in the nose, twin flexible .303in Brownings in the dorsal position and a single .303in Vickers K gun in the ventral position.

The basic Douglas DB-7 first flew in December 1938 and, although both fast and altogether modern, at that time its big

Right: Revealing study of a Mitchell II of 180 Squadron, July 1943. / *Aeroplane*

weakness was that the crew compartments were completely separated from one another, although the wireless operator/air gunner in the rear compartment could just see the pilot's back and pass messages to him by a pulley system if two inter-com systems and call light systems became u/s. Basic dual controls were installed in this rear compartment but were of no practical use.

Boston IIIs began to reach No 88 Squadron of 2 Group in mid-1941 and by January 1942 two more squadrons were equipping and training, Nos 226 and 107, and in February the type flew its first operational sorties when aircraft of 88 and 226 Squadrons were hurriedly ordered to help seek out and attack the *Scharnhorst* and *Gneisenau* during the German warships' famous dash through the English Channel. None of these sorties proved successful.

On 22 February four of 226's Bostons bombed enemy shipping off the Hook of Holland. Then, on 8 March, Bostons made their

first attack on a land target when 80 aircraft from 88 and 226 Squadrons bombed the Matford works at Poissy, near Paris. This was a deeper penetration than usual for our day bombers and the Bostons flew there and back at a very low level, seeing in the air on the outward trip to the target only three Ju88s some 2,000ft above them. Fortunately the Jus did not notice them, and the leading Boston, piloted by Wg Cdr Butler with Flg Off Sayers as navigator, reached the target exactly on time. The others followed and 10 direct hits were made on the factory before the bombers turned for home. Wg Cdr Butler's Boston, Z2206 G-George of 226 Squadron, seems to have been damaged either by bursting bombs, light flak or by colliding with something, for a few miles from the target it was seen to be in difficulties. Butler attempted to force land in a field but before reaching it he hit a tree with his port wing. The Boston hurtled across a field, hit the ground and exploded. With the

exception of its leader the attackers returned safely; landing at a Coastal Command airfield just as three Bf109s made an attack on it. They saw one of the enemy fighters shot down by the ground defences.

Five months later, Bostons played a prominent part in the air operations during the combined raid on Dieppe by laying smokescreens and close-support bombing. Their speed and improved armament was considerably better than the Blenheim's and they soon became popular with their crews, once the latter had become accustomed to the American bomber's relatively high landing speed. The Boston's bomb load was, in fact, twice that of the Blenheim and furthermore the battery of four fixed guns in the nose gave it an additional punch on low-level operations.

As a rule the Bostons operated in box formations of six to ten, with a strong fighter escort, on their daylight raids. They were nevertheless requently opposed by enemy fighters, but the escorting Spitfires were usually able to repel any attacks and relatively few Bostons were shot down.

Flak was another constant menace and the Bostons did not often return unscathed from many of their targets. To counter this, pilots were instructed by group to employ continually changing evasive tactics, such as losing height after attacking one day, and gaining height on another, a ploy which would upset predicted fire more than course changes of 30 degrees.

Yet another hazard was bird strikes, as exemplified by the experiences of two 88 Squadron Bostons during operations over France on 19 July 1942: one had its nose perspex broken in the observer's face resulting in the sortie having to be abandoned, and

Above left: Douglas Boston IIIs of 88 Squadron, first squadron to be equipped with the type. / *IWM*

Below left: A Lockheed Ventura I of 21 Squadron at its base in Norfolk.

Below: A Ventura and crew of 464 Squadron, RAAF. Note the aircraft's forward armament.

the other suffered a similar strike which injured the navigator/bomb aimer and forced the crew to abandon the attack on their primary target and bomb an alternative objective instead.

The Boston's bombing accuracy was found wanting at first, but an attempt to improve it by partly substituting the better, gyroscopically controlled Mk XIV bomb sight for the original Mk IX sights proved fruitless. Trouble was also encountered on the run up: the Bostons tended to porpoise and the remedial action adopted here was to open the doors well before reaching the target to allow time for trim adjustment.

A second version of the Boston III came into use during 1941, the A-20C, which had a combat range of 1,050 miles on 66 per cent power compared with the 800 miles of its forerunner. It could carry self-sealing bomb bay fuel tanks of 140 gallons capacity, had different radio and compass equipment and its twin dorsal guns were now of .30in calibre instead of .303in. Also, Douglas-built A-20Cs (but not Boeing-built examples) incorporated ejector type exhaust stacks on each cylinder in place of the collector ring assembly, a modification which conferred an increase of some 15mph in top speed. The modification also resulted in the heating system changing from steam to electrical, although the new exhaust system initially proved troublesome in service.

As recorded in more detail elsewhere in this book, 2 Group left Bomber Command at the end of May 1943. A few months beforehand, another version of the Boston began to reach the group's squadrons, where it gradually replaced the early aircraft. This was the Mk IIIA, exclusively Boeing-built and having the new ejector exhaust system as standard.

Deliveries to 107 and 226 Squadrons began in January 1943 followed by 88 Squadron in February, and by the end of March 74 had been flown to Britain from the USA. Meanwhile, as a result of heavy Blenheim V (RAF name 'Bisley') losses in North Africa, 2 Group's Boston squadrons had been told to relinquish their Boston IIIs so that these could be sent to that theatre of operations.

This, of course, seriously dislocated 2 Group's growing offensive, until the squadrons had re-equipped and trained on their new Boston IIIAs. For the record, the last Boston III bombing sorties flown by the group were made on 11 February by 88 and 226 Squadrons, the very final Mk III sorties of any sort occurring on 5 April when two A-20Cs made an unsuccessful search for group Ventura crews shot down during the previous day's operations.

Training on the Boston IIIAs continued until the end of April and the first operational sorties by the type came on 1 May, when box formations of 107 Squadron's aircraft set out to bomb Caen. Unfortunately, as quite often happened in 2 Group's daylight operations, the mission was rendered abortive because the target was completely obscured by cloud.

During April, No 342 (Free French) Squadron formed in 2 Group from what had hitherto been known solely as the 'Lorraine' Squadron, and it received Boston IIIAs. However, it did not become operational until June, by which time 2 Group was no longer in Bomber Command.

At the end of May 1942 a second type of American twin-engined light bomber joined 2 Group, the porcine Lockheed Vega Ventura, which had been developed from the larger Model 18 Lodestar airliner to meet an RAF requirement and first ordered in February 1940. It was built by Lockheed's subsidiary company Vega, which also built Boeing B-17 Fortresses, and the prototype, AE658, first flew on 31 July 1941. In appearance the Ventura closely resembled the Lockheed Model 14 Hudson, which had entered service with RAF Coastal Command in 1939, although compared with the older aircraft, the Ventura had its bulbous, twin .303in Browning-armed Boulton-Paul dorsal turret further forward to allow a better field of fire. It also featured a 'stepped' underside to the rear fuselage to accommodate a gun position armed with two more .303in guns. Nose armament comprised two fixed .50in guns and two movable .303s. Maximum bomb load was 2,500lb and the type's two Pratt & Whitney Double Wasp GR 2800 engines gave it a top speed of 300mph and a cruising speed of 260mph.

2 Group crews wondered what the new bomber would do that the Hudson wouldn't, and it was not long before they found out: little, if anything, except consume more fuel!

21 Squadron was the first to re-equip with the 'Flying Pig' or just 'Pig', as it was invariably dubbed by 2 Group's crews, and eventually two more joined it, 487 (RNZAF) and 464 (RAAF) Squadrons; the three, all of whom were based in Norfolk, jointly formed a wing. The Ventura was chosen to replace the Blenheim IV as a short-range night intruder, a task which the Bristol type had been compelled to undertake increasingly due to heavy losses in daylight operations, but although some night intruder training was undertaken the Ventura's role was changed to day bombing before

it finally went into action. Teething troubles suffered by the Venturas following their arrival in Britain included leaking fuel tanks and seizing vacuum pumps; also the navigator's station proved unsatisfactory, this accordingly being altered on all aircraft by a civilian contractor.

Ventura crews comprised a pilot, navigator, wireless operator and straight gunner. The Ventura Wing completed crew and formation training by the end of November, and then stood by for a week awaiting an important daylight attack on the Philips radio and valve works at Eindhoven in Holland which was responsible for almost a third of Germany's supply of radio components. The Venturas formed part of a mixed force of 90 light bombers, the other types being Bostons and Mosquitos, which took off shortly before noon on 6 December 1942 on what was to be 2 Group's most notable operation of the whole year.

The Bostons led the raid, followed by the Mosquitos and, lastly, the three Ventura squadrons carrying a mixture of incendiary and delayed action HE bombs. At times visibility over the North Sea was reduced to one mile by rain squalls, but despite cloud as low as 200 feet the raiders pressed on at very low level and the majority succeeded in reaching the objective. The attack lasted ten minutes and the last crews reported many fires and billowing smoke in the target area, and subsequent photo reconnaissance confirmed that heavy damage had been done to the factory. Furthermore, only minor damage was done to civilian property and the raid acted as a symbol to intensify passive resistance of Dutchmen towards the local German administrators.

But both near Eindhoven and during the return trip the bombers were subjected to both flak and fighter attacks, with the result that 13 aircraft failed to return, four Bostons (three of which are known to have fallen to fighters), one Mosquito and nine Venturas, including that flown by the CO of 487 Squadron. Many bombers came home bearing battle scars and several had wounded among their crews. There were also some narrow escapes. One New Zealand pilot saw the Ventura flying alongside him blown to pieces. Another Ventura was hit by flak which set alight some Very cartridges, filling the bomber with thick, acrid smoke before they were finally extinguished. Several aircraft had their Perspex windows or wing fabric damaged by seagulls and ducks, and one New Zealand Ventura had its nose damaged by a tree as it tried to get away at low level after bombing.

Following this raid the Venturas joined 2 Group's other light bombers in the task of attacking fringe targets with fighter escort. These 'Circus' operations were made by relatively small numbers of bombers, escorted by numerous fighters. They required only brief penetration of enemy territory and were normally executed by one or two bomber squadrons. The Venturas would cross the Channel

Above left: Venturas of 21 Squadron in two vics of three, January 1943. The Ventura's porcine fuselage resulted in it being nicknamed the 'Flying Pig'. /*Aeroplane*

Above: Mitchell IIs of 180 Squadron flying in formation above the clouds in July 1943. /*Aeroplane*

in close formation at 'nought feet' to elude the enemy's early warning radar and then climb quickly to their bombing height of 10,000ft, swiftly diving for 'the deck' again after their attack and leaving their escort to prevent any pursuit. In daylight attacks delivered in the period January to 31 May 1943, actual losses were light (1.2 per cent of sorties) on these tip-and-run raids, but on many occasions some of the Venturas were badly damaged although they returned safely. Because of this apparent ability to withstand heavy battle damage and still fly, the 'Pig' endeared itself to its crews, but even so it was not an outstanding success as a day bomber. It was too slow and not sufficiently well armed to withstand fighter attack, as was emphasised disastrously on 3 May, when 11 Venturas of 487 Squadron set out to attack Amsterdam power station, failed to rendezvous with RAF fighters and lost all but one of their number in a running battle with enemy fighters. Among the unlucky Venturas was AJ209 flown by Sqn Ldr L. H. Trent, 487's CO, who, when the full story of his gallantry was finally pieced together at the end of the war, was awarded the Victoria Cross.

Last of the trio of American 'twins' to join 2 Group was the North American Mitchell, named after General Billy Mitchell, outspoken pioneer of US military aviation. Developed from the NA-40 attack bomber of 1938, the first B-25 for the US Army Air Corps flew in August 1940 and the second basic model, the B-25B, became the first to be supplied to the RAF, as the Mitchell I. Only a few of these were delivered and none was used operationally, the main version for the RAF being the Mk II, counterpart of the USAAF's B-25C and D.

A light bomber with a crew of five, the Mitchell I had a span of 67ft 6¾in, was 54ft 1in long and was powered by two Wright Double-Row Cyclone engines. Top speed was 292mph at 15,000ft, cruising speed 210mph and range 1,640 miles with 4,000lb of bombs or 950 miles with maximum bomb load of 6,000lb. Defensive armament comprised a single hand-held .50in nose gun, plus two .50in guns in the dorsal turret and two more in the retractable ventral turret.

Mitchell II production started with FL164 but the first example to reach 2 Group was FL179 which arrived at Bodney on 16 July 1942. It was delivered to 21 Squadron which was, at the time, in the throes of re-equipping with Venturas, but after a few days at

Bodney it, and two more of its kind which had followed, were transferred to West Raynham for Nos 98 and 180 Squadrons, both of whom formed there early in September. Primary roles of the Mitchells were to be Circus and Ramrod operations the latter being similar to Circus except that its principal objective was the destruction of the target and army support. Secondary roles were low level attacks on land objectives, attacks on important shipping, and short range night bombing. During the squadrons' work-up period, gun-jamming problems frequently arose after firing about a dozen rounds, but by January the problem seemed to have been cured and on 22 January the first operation was mounted by 98 and 180 Squadrons. Each unit put up six aircraft, each armed with two 1,000lb MC and four 500lb MC bombs, to bomb oil tanks and an oil refinery alongside the Ghent-Terneuzen canal in Belgium. En route one aircraft had to return because the pilot's face was badly cut as a result of a bird strike. As the remainder neared the target they climbed to 1,500 feet but heavy, accurate flak was soon encountered and one aircraft was destroyed by a direct hit. The targets were bombed and hit but the Mitchell flown by the CO of 180 Squadron was set on fire by flak and finished off by Fw190s, which also sent another Mitchell into the sea. Fortunately, a squadron of Mustangs soon arrived on the scene and drove the attackers away, but not until another Mitchell had suffered six damaging attacks.

In mid-March a third Mitchell squadron formed in 2 Group when No 320 (Dutch) Squadron was transferred from Coastal Command to re-equip with the North American light bomber. Most of its original Mitchells were paid for by the Dutch government. Meanwhile, gun problems had reappeared in 98 and 180 Squadrons and they had mainly been preoccupied with modification programmes, practice Circuses and, as a further part of their continuing training, air-sea rescue sorties. Mitchell offensive operations were finally resumed on 11 May when aircraft of 180 Squadron attacked Boulogne marshalling yards, the first of seven Mitchell raids made during that month. On 25 May when 180 Squadron attacked the Luftwaffe fighter base at Abbeville, the formation leader's Mitchell was hit by flak during the run-up. Pieces fell away and damaged another Mitchell, forcing it to dive for safety. Flak was again heavy when 98 and 180 Squadrons each sent six Mitchells to bomb Flushing on the final day of the month, one machine being forced down in the sea off Clacton. This brought the Mitchell's career with Bomber Command to an end, for 2 Group was now to come under new ownership as already mentioned. The Mitchell's ability to carry thousand-pounders had been an advantage of 2 Group, but on the other hand, from the flying point of view, the gull-winged bomber lacked the manoeuvrability of that other fine American light twin, the Boston.

Super Stirling (B.8/41)

By late 1941 the Short Stirling heavy bomber was well-established in service and was generally proving to be a satisfactory aircraft. It represented a big increase in hitting power, it was more manoeuvrable than any other bomber of its size and, in spite of being unforgiving of careless handling on take-off, it was generally well-liked by its crews. Due to the limitations imposed by the original specification, B.12/36, the Stirling did have two serious drawbacks which were eventually to cause its replacement as a heavy night bomber: due to its low-aspect ratio wing its cruising height was low enough to make it very vulnerable to AA fire, and it could not carry the latest heavy bombs, the bomb bay being designed to accommodate large numbers of comparatively small bombs.

Faced with the possible demise of the Stirling in favour of the Lancaster and Halifax, Short Bros prepared a development of their big bomber which would eliminate the undesirable features of the design. The new bomber, given the Short Bros design number S.36, was designed to Specification B.8/41 and was considerably larger than the Stirling. Powered by four Bristol Centaurus 18-cylinder sleeve-valve engines of over 2,000hp each, it was expected to have a normal loaded weight of 80,000lb, with 103,100lb maximum over-load weight. To overcome the earlier height problems the S.36 had an aspect ratio of 8.62 and wing span of 136ft.

The original Stirling bomb bay, divided into individual cells for 500lb bombs or 2,000lb AP bombs of similar diameter, was replaced by a new, unobstructed bay capable of housing up to six 4,000lb HC bombs. Six additional wing cells could carry 1,000lb bombs, bringing the maximum bomb load up to 30,000lb. Other possible fuselage loads were 12 x 1,000lb GP bombs, nine 1,900lb bombs, nine 2,000lb bombs, or one 8,000lb HC bomb and two-thirds of the smaller bomb loads in the front and rear sections. The six 1,000lb bombs in the wings could be carried with all the alternative fuselage loads. Typical bomb load/range was 12,000lb of bombs carried for 2,000 miles at 221mph, but over a range of 3,000 miles at the same cruising speed the bomb load was reduced to 1,000lb; this, however, was well beyond the normal radius of operations and would only have been necessary for a special mission.

At 80,000lb weight, the Short B.8/41 could be expected to attain a maximum level speed of 282mph at 3,250ft ('M' blower setting) and 311mph at 20,000ft ('S' blower setting). At 103,100lb these figures were reduced to 275mph and 300mph respectively.

On max economical cruise power at 80,000lb weight the new bomber was expected to attain 243mph at 6,500ft ('M' blower) and 262mph at 24,000ft ('S' blower). The figures at 103,100lb were 234 mph and 237mph respectively. Defensive armament was to consist of two .5in guns in the nose turret, four .5in guns in the mid-upper turret, two .303in guns in the under turret and four .5in guns in the tail turret.

The Air Ministry RTD.1 figures for the new bomber varied slightly from those estimated by Short Brothers, giving slightly

Below: Short B.8/41 (S.36) 'Super Stirling' with four Bristol Centaurus engines.

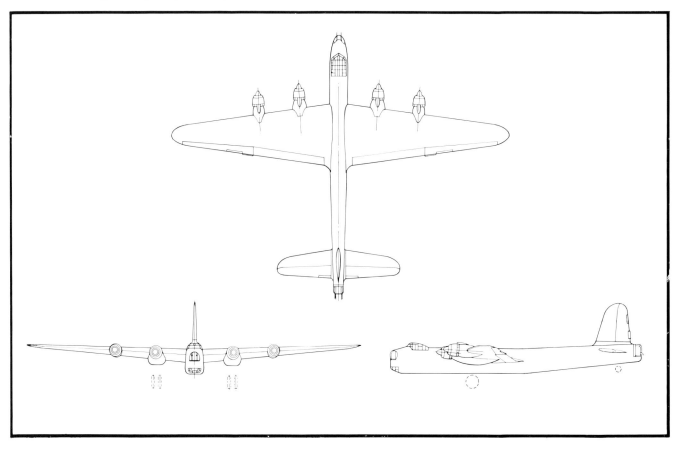

reduced maximum and cruising speeds but increased range. For example, at an economical speed of 190mph, 1,000lb of bombs could be carried for 3,300 miles. Weak mixture cruise speed was given as 214mph at 15,000ft for 2,120 miles, carrying 12,000lb of bombs. The Air Staff and RAF were very enthusiastic about the new project and considered that it would be the next logical development in heavy bomber hitting power, and the first prototype was expected to fly in September 1943. Unfortunately, the Centaurus CE3SM engines, driving 15ft 3in propellers, proved to be incapable of giving the required cruising power at 19,000-24,000ft as had originally been expected. Their maximum cruising height was 15,000ft, much the same as that of the Stirling, which had come in for so much criticism.

Because of this reduced height, in the vulnerable gun and fighter region, the RAF insisted on much heavier armour protection, amounting to some 9,000lb, to protect the crews and vital parts of the aircraft. This had the effect of reducing bomb load/range figures. The whole project began to look less attractive, and the massive re-organisation and change-over in production that the B.8/41 would have required made the Ministry of Aircraft Production disapprove of the whole programme. It was unlikely that any Short B.8/41s could reach the squadrons before mid-1944. The Bomber Command planners still wanted the Super Stirling, as it became known, because of its increased hitting capability, but those responsible for ensuring the constant flow of replacement aircraft for the RAF saw the aircraft as a hindrance. They felt that the cessation of Stirling production in favour of B.8/41s would produce an unjustified time lag before new bombers could flow from production lines. There would be a loss of several hundred Stirlings from the factories during the change-over and it would only be possible to produce two B.8/41s to every three Stirlings. They argued that the hitting power of three Stirlings was greater than two B.8/41s, but this line of thought totally ignored the fact that the B.8/41 could devastate areas with 4,000lb and 8,000 bombs instead of the small bombs used by the Stirling.

After considerable argument, during which Short Bros also pointed out the advantages of the Super Stirling, the production planners won the day and the B.8/41 was cancelled. Some of the arguments in favour of abandoning the B.8/41 programme were valid: production of the big bomber would certainly have had a detrimental effect on Stirling production and Short's earlier aircraft was required, not only as a night bomber, but also as a glider tug and transport. With the Halifax and Lancaster, and other new heavy bomber projects under development, the RAF needs in this field were adequately covered without the need for another bomber at that time. Had it been put into production the B.8/41 would not have played a significant part in Bomber Command's offensive because it could not have reached many squadrons before the war ended. If it could have been got into operational service during 1943 it could have greatly increased the effectiveness of the RAF's night attacks, and its heavy defensive armament would have made it a formidable opponent for the German night fighter force.

The Mosquito Replacement

During 1941 the de Havilland Mosquito was just beginning to show its potential in service by virtue of its unique high performance, which made it officially the fastest combat aircraft in operational use with any nation. The Air Staff, however, were not entirely convinced that the Mosquito could continue to penetrate the enemy's defences by evading opposing fighters by sheer speed alone, especially as new and faster enemy fighters were bound to come into service. Bomber Command philosophy on the subject of bomber types favoured three distinct classes: the very fast unarmed light bomber/reconnaissance aircraft, the heavily-armed light day bomber with moderate performance, and the very heavy, fairly slow night bomber. The first two classes would operate at medium and low altitudes, often in attacks on specialised pin-point targets or in support of ground forces, but the heavy night bomber would operate at increasingly high altitudes.

The heavily-armed day bomber was to be the Bristol Buckingham, but the requirement for the very high speed unarmed light bomber envisaged development of a new type to increase performance beyond that attained by the Mosquito as currently in service. To this end the Air Staff drew up Specification B.11/41 for a high speed bomber of medium size powered by two Napier Sabre engines, with Bristol Centaurus as alternatives.

The primary contractor for the new bomber was to be Hawkers, then actively engaged on development and production of the Typhoon. The B.11/41 was required to carry a bomb load of 4,000lb, to attain a maximum speed at 25,000ft of not less than 400mph and to cruise at 20,000ft at not less than 330mph on weak mixture at max cruise power. It was to be able to carry 4,000lb of bombs on internal fuel for not less than 1,600 miles, to fly for 1,775 miles without bombs on internal fuel and to have a range of 2,500 miles with auxiliary tanks in the bomb bay. On take-off the B.11/41 had to be able to clear a 50ft obstacle after a run of 850yd from a grass field when carrying 4,000lb of bombs and fuel for 1,600 milers.

When first in service it was intended that the new bomber should be unarmed and rely on its performance, but it was felt that provision should be made for it to have a mid-upper turret, housing either two .5in or four .303in guns, if opposing fighters began to match it in speed.

The new bomber had to be capable of carrying a versatile selection of bombs, from small bomb containers to a single 4,000lb HC bomb. The B.11/41 design also had to be capable of conversion into a long-range fighter by substitution of the bomber nose for a fighter nose carrying six 20mm guns.

Sydney Camm, Hawker's Chief Designer, designed a clean, mid-wing monoplane, powered by two Sabres, to meet the specification. Of all-metal construction the new bomber had a wing span of 70ft and an estimated max weight as a bomber of 30,000lb. At a normal cruising speed of 345mph Hawkers estimated that the range with a 4,000lb bomb load would be 1,130 miles, but at economical cruise power and 242mph the range of 1,600 miles could be achieved.

Hawker's expected the maximum speed to be 420mph on the power of two Napier Sabre NS8SM engines and the service ceiling was estimated to be 36,000ft.

Maximum loaded weight of the new bomber was estimated by Hawkers to be 30,000lb, although the Air Ministry's own estimate put the weight at 32,000lb, with all the performance figures slightly lower as a result (every tendered design was closely scrutinised by the Ministry's technical staff to check the feasibility of a company's performance, weight and drag estimates, and it was not unusual for the AM figures to be somewhat pessimistic). Hawker's estimate of the speed attained by the fighter version armed with six 20mm guns was 420mph, with an economical cruise speed of 242mph.

At the end of 1941 two Hawker B.11/41s were ordered for prototype development, these having the serial numbers HV266 and HV270.

Early in 1942 a full-scale wooden mock-up of the bomber was completed and a conference on the aircraft and inspection of the mock-up was held at Hawkers' Kingston-on-Thames factory on 27 February. Progress was such that the Air Ministry provisionally ordered 200 examples of the bomber to get production under way, with further orders intended, and the aircraft was expected to become one of the RAF's major new types.

In the meantime de Havilland's had projected a scaled-up Mosquito, powered by Napier Sabre engines and of all-wood construction, to meet the same specification, but at first the Air Ministry were reluctant to allow de Havillands to become involved in the new high speed bomber programme because of diverting their attention from other urgent work, including Mosquito development, the single-engined jet fighter, the Hornet and a new high-speed night fighter. After much thought and discussion, such importance was attached to developing a new high-speed replacement for the Mosquito that a decision was taken to put both the Hawker and de Havilland B.11/41s into production, and in consequence find ways of stepping up Napier Sabre production, if necessary by starting new production lines in Canada and America. It was considered that it could be an advantage to have both all-metal and all-wood airframes in service in case of problems with either under extreme conditions overseas. The all-wood aircraft structure, as related to high-performance aircraft such as the Mosquito, had yet to be extensively tested in tropical conditions at that time.

Miles Aircraft too produced a project to meet Specification B.11/41, an unorthodox tandem-wing twin-engined aircraft with the main wing at the rear and a fore-plane for longitudinal control. To test the design a ⅝th scale flying model of the bomber, powered by two de Havilland Gipsy Majors and designated M.39B, was built and successfully flown. Although the full-scale bomber was not built, the M.39B gave valuable data on the design of tandem-wing aeroplanes.

De Havilland's B.11/41, powered by two Napier Sabre NS8SM engines, was expected to have a top speed of 392mph and to cruise at 300mph. With the later NS19S1M version of the big 24-cylinder engine it was estimated to attain 430mph and cruise at 328mph.

Generally an enlarged Mosquito of approximately 70ft span and carrying a crew of three, the DH B.11/41 was, like the Hawker design, intended to carry bombs of various sizes up to a single 4,000lb HC 'cookie' in the internal bay.

The RAF was enthusiastic about getting the B.11/41s into service as soon as possible, but the whole programme became beset

Right: Hawker B.11/41 (P.1005) twin-engined high-speed bomber with two Napier Sabre engines.

with difficulties. The Sabre engine, much-favoured by designers of the second generation fighters and their developments, was required in quantity for the Typhoon, Tempest and Firebrand, but problems in development were delaying the production and supply of this engine. The Typhoon was starting to come into service and as great hopes were attached to the new fighter it was imperative that nothing should interrupt the flow of Sabre engines to the factories. Massive production of the Tempest was also expected, and the introduction of two B.11/41s into production, each example using two of the much-needed engines, posed a major problem of supply.

One serious suggestion was that Hawker B.11/41s should be produced in quantity without engines and, if urgently required, should be engined with Sabres removed from Typhoons; but there was no any indication of what action could be taken if B.11/41s and Typhoons were urgently required at the same time! Increased production of the Sabre, with factories working a 24-hour day, was the only solution. The B.11/41 airframes were no less a problem: de Havilland's factories were fully engaged on Mosquito production of bomber, trainer and fighter variants. Hawker were working to full capacity on Typhoon and Tempest production. The Hawker B.11/41 was always considered to be the primary design in the 'Mosquito replacement' programme, and even if the de Havilland design was dropped the Hawker bomber (designated Hawker P.1005) was still considered by the Air Ministry as an urgently required aircraft. The engine supply problem could have been eased by re-designing the aircraft to be powered by two Bristol Centaurus engines, but probably at the expense of a reduced performance. Projects were undertaken for later variants of the Hawker B.11/41 with turbojet engines, but these were intended as developments for later years.

At this time the development by Rolls-Royce of the Merlin 60 series two-stage two-speed engines, intended to give greatly increased power at higher altitudes than existing Merlins, had raised Spitfire performance to over 400mph and there was expectation that installation of this mark of Merlin in the Mosquito could increase its already impressive performance in the same way. Installation of Merlin 61s in the original prototype, W4050, was undertaken in October 1941, and engine runs with the new

powerplants commenced on 17 June 1942. Flight trials soon confirmed the expected increase in performance when on 23 July a speed of 432mph was recorded. With Merlin 77 engines this prototype recorded a speed of 437mph in December, the highest ever attained by a Mosquito. The Mosquito B.IX, the first production bomber with Merlin 61 series engines, attained a maximum level speed of 424mph at 26,200ft. Later a pressure cabin enabled the Mosquito to operate at increasing height and the increased engine power and modifications to the bomb bay and doors enabled the bomb load to be increased to 4,000lb including the carriage of a single 4,000lb HC bomb. Thus, development of the production Mosquito had met most of the requirements of Specification B.11/41, and in a smaller airframe with a crew of two.

The problems with supply of Sabres had not been resolved and it seemed impossible to find any production space and capacity within the industry to cope with production of the Hawker B.11/41 bomber. All companies were full to capacity with work, with the possible exception of Vickers-Armstrongs at Weybridge, who were not, however, geared to stressed-skin aeroplanes, having produced a series of geodetic types. Vickers still had plenty of Wellington and Warwick work, but were looking for new work to follow. They hoped that orders would be placed for their new geodetic projects.

In view of the difficulty in finding production capacity for increased Sabre production and the airframes, and the development of the Mosquito up to the type of performance and load-carrying ability required by Specification B.11/41, the Air Ministry reluctantly cancelled all further work on the Hawker bomber. In their letter to Hawkers the Ministry stressed that their decision did not reflect any doubts about the excellence of the design, but was taken purely because of production difficulties.

The Hawker P.1005 seemed to be a design of great potential and had it been brought into service quickly it might have become one of the outstanding aircraft of World War II. In addition to its bomber role it could probably have been developed into a high-speed night fighter. In its later developments it could have become the RAF's first jet bomber, pre-dating the Canberra by several years and providing valuable experience for crews until that excellent twin-jet bomber was available.

The Vickers B.5/41

During the last two years prior to the outbreak of World War II the Air Staff were much attracted to the potential of the bomber flying at very high altitudes, which made it almost immune from interception. They had already asked Vickers to investigate the possibility of producing a version of the Wellington with a pressure cabin, which had resulted in the experimental Mk V prototypes powered by Bristol Hercules engines giving maximum power at great heights. Further development of the pressure-cabin Wellington, powered by Rolls-Royce Merlin 60 high-altitude engines, produced the Mk VI, which was placed in production. On these two marks of Wellington installation of the pressure cabin capsule had been successfully married to the basic geodetic fuselage structure, and these aircraft were able to operate at heights around 40,000ft. The Air Staff were convinced that the very high-altitude heavy bomber could penetrate deep into enemy airspace almost immune from fighter attack and anti-aircraft fire, but their policy also required that any planned future bomber should be able to carry a worthwhile bomb load over a long range when employed on strategic bombing. To bring these requirements together Specification B.5/41 was issued, which called for the design of a heavy bomber to carry a bomb load of 8,000lb over a range of 2,000 miles, approaching the target at 38,000ft and returning from the target, after dropping the bomb load, at 40,000ft. Auxiliary tanks were to give the bomber a range of 2,350 miles with a 6,000lb bomb load, and a maximum speed of 345mph was required.

Any design to meet this Specification had to be large and powered by a minimum of four engines capable of giving high power at the extreme altitudes mentioned. Vickers' success in producing the pressure-cabin versions of the Wellington led Rex Pierson, their Chief Designer, to use the Warwick fuselage, incorporating the pressure-cabin capsule, as an initial basis for a new four-engined bomber to meet the B.5/41 requirement. Known provisionally as the Warwick III (although little of the Warwick remained) the new bomber was powered by four Rolls-Royce Merlin 60-series engines mounted on an elliptical wing of high

aspect ratio. The early projects of the Warwick III had the conventional two-wheel main undercarriage of the standard Warwick layout. This was, however, now discarded in favour of a revival of the four-main-wheel system projected for the earlier Vickers B.12/36 and B.1/39 designs, in which each separate nacelle housed a main undercarriage leg and wheel to spread the aircraft weight along the wing span when the aircraft was on the ground. Like the Wellington VI it was intended that the only defensive armament should be a single pressurised turret in the tail housing four .303 Browning guns, pressurisation being effected by the cabin air control system. It is probable, however, that a remote control system, as finally adopted for the Wellington Mk VI, would have been used.

The Vickers B.5/41 was estimated to have a maximum speed of 351mph at 32,000ft and to carry an 8,000lb bomb load to a target at 37,000ft. It was estimated to take 40 minutes to reach operational ceiling. Range with 8,000lb of bombs was expected to be 1,850 miles, but with the bomb load reduced to 6,300lb the B.5/41 had an estimated range of 2,160 miles. The Vickers B.5/41 design carried a pilot, navigator, wireless operator and observer/gunner, and weighed 50,000lb fully loaded. Four Merlin 60 engines were specified as the primary installation, but Hercules high-altitude radial engines were an alternative.

The new four-engined bomber was given the Vickers type number 433 and two prototypes, DW506 and DW512, were ordered for evaluation.

As the design progressed doubts made the Air Staff review policy in regard to high-altitude bombing. It seemed unlikely that an acceptable degree of accuracy could be obtained with bombing from extreme heights, and the effect of high altitude on the working efficiency of crews was an unknown factor at that time. The only experience that the RAF had acquired of bombing from 30,000ft or thereabouts had been with the Fortress 1s of No 90 Squadron and the results had been discouraging. Many problems had been encountered and a high proportion of the bombs dropped had fallen wide of the target area when released from around 30,000ft — and the B.5/41 bomber was planned to bomb from 38,000ft. In view of all the problems and unknowns it was considered unwise to proceed further with development of a large and costly aeroplane tailored purely for the specialised high-altitude bombing role. The Vickers B.5/41 was therefore abandoned, but features of the design, such as the wing, nacelles and tail unit, were later revived for the Vickers B.3/42 project. This became the Windsor and the serial numbers of the two B.5/41 prototypes. DW506 and DW512, were transferred to the first two Windsor prototypes.

Below: Vickers B.5/41 high-altitude bomber.

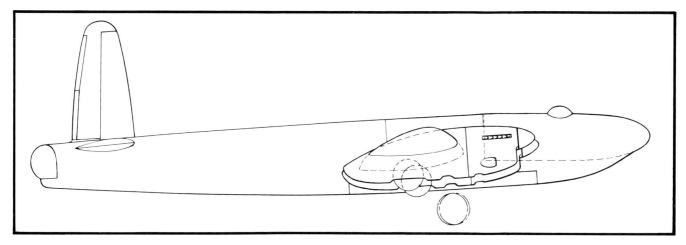

The Vickers Windsor

By the end of 1941 the factories of Vickers-Armstrong posed a major problem for Ministry of Aircraft Production planning for future production. For many years Vickers had produced a succession of geodetic aeroplanes and all the factory departments were geared to this type of construction. The company was naturally reluctant to discard what was a proven constructional method and unwilling to undertake the major upheaval of re-organising the factories to manufacture conventional stressed-skin aircraft. The Wellesley had been followed in production by the Wellington and Warwick and it is true to say that the latter bomber would not have been persevered with if it had not had goedetic construction. The Warwick was not going to be produced in the numbers originally considered and by the beginning of 1942 the Wellington was clearly nearing the end of its operational career as the principal twin-engined night bomber. Attempts to adapt the Wellington for another operational role and to find an operational bomber role for the Warwick had resulted in the developments of the very high altitude versions of these types, the production Mk VI pressure-cabin version of the Wellington and the so-called 'Warwick III' four-engined pressurised bomber project, of which two prototypes were on order. If a new type was not forthcoming, it seemed, with the expected run-down in Wellington production, that Vickers' factories could be without work by 1943 or 1944.

The Bristol Buckingham at the beginning of 1942 was considered by the RAF to be an urgently required type to replace existing light bombers and large numbers of the type would have to be produced. Bristols were faced with the problem of finding factory space for the Buckingham without disrupting Beaufighter and Beaufort production, and clearly this would have been an ideal aircraft for Vickers to produce if their factories had been equipped to manufacture stressed-skin designs. It was even suggested that Vickers should produce a geodetic version of the Buckingham, and although this did not receive serious consideration, it did lead to thoughts of the type of 'Wellington replacement' that Vickers might design and which would be required by the RAF in large numbers. Using the idea of a 'geodetic Buckingham' type of bomber, Rex Pierson designed a medium-sized day or night bomber, under the designation RKP/61735, powered by two Bristol Centaurus engines. Although this project could carry a 4,000lb bomb load for 1,550 miles, which was similar to the Buckingham, it differed in carrying a maximum bomb load of 8,000lb, twice that of the Bristol aircraft. Maximum speed was 353mph at 23,500ft, weak mixture cruising speed 283mph and most economical cruising speed 246mph. Reinforcing range, without bomb load, was 2,700 miles.

This project had a close affinity to the Buckingham and in order to obtain first-hand information about it Rex Pierson visited the Bristol Company at Filton to inspect the mock-up and see the installation of the Centaurus engines. Bristol made Buckingham data available to Rex Pierson to assist him in his design. It was suggested that the Buckingham engine installation could be made available for the Vickers design. Because of its ability to carry twice the bomb load of the Bristol or Hawker bombers Rex Pierson's bomber was somewhat larger, particularly in span. Its overall performance was close to the Buckingham's, but it was 50mph slower than the Hawker bomber in maximum and cruising speeds. Its all-up weight was 37,500lb. The total defensive armament consisted of two .5in guns mounted in barbettes in the end of each nacelle, remotely controlled and fired from a central sighting position in the tail.

The new Vickers bomber was the subject of a searching detailed examination by the Air Staff and the Research and Development departments of the Air Ministry. The new design showed little advantage over existing new types, except that it could be produced at Vickers factories. Although it was similar in performance to the Buckingham and it carried the same bomb load as the Vickers Warwick, the new bomber could only carry that load for 550 miles instead of 1,620 miles.

The Air Staff were critical of the armament layout and considered it quite unacceptable because in certain blind spots a maximum of only two .5in guns could be brought to bear on an attacking fighter.

The Research and Development Departments of the Air Ministry drafted several alternative designs to see what could be achieved and after considering several layouts suggested to Vickers that a more attractive and advanced design could result from installation of four Rolls-Royce Merlin 60 engines in a larger airframe, which would give higher speed and carry a bigger bomb load over longer range. Vickers' design office was already engaged on detailed structural design of the company's B.5/41 four-Merlin high altitude bomber and project drafts soon showed Rex Pierson that major components of this design could be utilised in the redesign of the 'Wellington replacement' bomber with four Merlins. Using the existing wing, nacelles and tail unit, but redesigning the fuselage to meet the differing operational requirement produced a much more attractive and potent proposal than the earlier twin-

Above: Fine study of the third prototype Windsor on test. Outer nacelles are designed to house barbettes but they have not yet been installed.

Centaurus aeroplane. The new fuselage was deeper than on the B.5/41 and the pressure cabin capsule was replaced by conventional crew positions, but a feature of the design, to reduce drag, was the provision for only one pilot housed in a small and restricted fighter-type cockpit, with limited access from the rest of the aircraft — an unusual and controversial feature in so large an aeroplane.

Specification B.3/42 was drafted around the new Vickers bomber, which was given the type number 447 and the official name Windsor Mk 1.

At the early stage in the design of the B.3/42 the all-up weight was estimated to be 55,000lb, and although the maximum bomb load remained the original 8,000lb of the twin-Centaurus design, the new bomber could carry this load for 1,400 miles when powered by four Merlin 61 engines. At a normal cruising speed of 315mph 4,000lb of bombs could be carried for 1,600 miles, similar figures to those of the original twin-engined design but at considerably higher speed. The same bomb load could be carried for 2,150 miles provided that the cruise speed was reduced to 240mph, the most economical speed. Maximum cruise speed was 330mph at 23,000ft.

Defensive armament for the Windsor caused considerable discussion, controversy, drafting of different schemes and changes of policy. The original scheme was for two .303in guns to be mounted in the nose with only limited movement to deter head-on attacks, and a rear turret, mounted aft of the fin and rudder, housing four .5in guns. Other turrets were also investigated beside the originally-projected Nash and Thomson four .303in gun design, which included two different Vickers turrets, each housing four .5in guns and a Bristol turret with four .5in guns.

In August 1942 the armament was established as two fixed .303in guns firing forward in the nose and a turret in the extreme rear of the fuselage housing two 20mm cannon, but the Air Staff became interested in reviving the idea of barbette armament, with remote control sighting, as on the original twin-engined design. Development of barbettes in the ends of nacelles had been continued at Vickers and an installation for the Windsor had been designed to have two 20mm guns housed in the end of each outer nacelle, with a sighting position in the tail in place of the existing turret. The development of remotely-controlled 20mm guns seemed to offer big advantages for warding off the attacks by cannon-armed night fighters which were now being encountered over Germany in large numbers. Not only was the weight of fire of cannon armament increased by the barbette installation, but the gunner in the sighting position was less vulnerable to a night fighter firing at the flashes of the bomber's armament.

On 15 February 1943 the decision was taken to adopt the barbette armament as standard, with the two fixed nose guns retained. In order to test the system, the second prototype Vickers Warwick, L9704, was equipped with a barbette in the end of each nacelle housing two .5in guns, a similar installation to that designed for the original twin-Centaurus bomber 'Wellington replacement'. It is probable that the smaller gun installation was used for the tests because the major design work had already been done, and this was the quickest way of getting air firing trials under way in order to obtain installation data for the larger weapons in the Windsor. The weight of the barbettes and guns was such that, in spite of the removal of the rear four-gun turret, problems were raised over the centre of gravity, and in order to bring this back to the correct position either the internal equipment and crew arrangements would have to be re-arranged or the nose would have to be lengthened. Vickers favoured the latter solution and it is thought that this may have been incorporated in the barbette-equipped third prototype, NK136.

Flexibility of the structure proved to be another problem of the

Windsor; the wings flexed so much in flight that they were designed with several degrees of droop when the aircraft was at rest on the undercarriage, the wing taking up the correct amount of dihedral for stability under normal flight loads. Twisting and flexing of the rear fuselage proved to be excessive and following accidents to Lancasters shedding fins during evasive action, the stress factors on the fuselage of the Windsor were increased and four longerons were incorporated into the fuselage structure instead of three as originally provided. The first two prototypes, taken over from the B.5/41 project, were too far advanced for these structural improvements to be incorporated, but the third prototype had the redesigned fuselage. The first two prototypes were thus flown to lower limits than the third, NK136. (NK136 had been ordered as the third prototype Windsor on 11 November 1942, under the revised Specification B.12/42 incorporating the armament and structural changes.)

Starting its design life at 55,000lb, the weight of the Windsor was now increasing at a steady rate as the aircraft became more fitted for an operational career. At this stage the production-type Windsor, with strengthened airframe, beam barbettes, and increased armour and internal equipment weighed an estimated 60,300lb, and 68,000lb in overload condition, at which weights the maximum speeds were expected to be 345mph and 339mph respectively. The cruising speeds were expected to be 320mph at 60,300lb and 318mph at 68,000lb. By now the maximum bomb load had increased to 12,000lb. At 325mph the maximum bomb load could be carried for 800 miles, 8,000lb could be carried for 1,300 miles and 4,000lb for 1,810 miles. At the economical speed of 230mph, a more realistic speed, the ranges could be increased to 1,060 miles, 1,740 miles and 2,410 miles respectively.

Powered by four Rolls-Royce Merlin RM14SM universal engines of increased power, the production-type Windsor was originally expected to attain about 380mph at 23,000ft at the same weights. Maximum cruising speeds were 317-321mph according to weight. At 230mph 4,000lb of bombs could be carried for 2,550 miles and 12,000lb for 1,470 miles. The Air Ministry Directorate of Technical Development check on these figures suggested that they were a little too high.

As construction of the first prototype progressed the all-up weight continued to rise and a new estimate put it at 71,821lb, which reduced the maximum speed to 363mph and cruising speeds to 303-308mph. The continual rise in weight was not only due to specification changes: Dr Barnes Wallis had not been able to give his close attention to the Windsor structure, due to other commitments, and there had been a lack of supervision on weight control. In order to prevent further steep rises in weight Vickers set up a weight control department, which could examine structural design and keep weight of components down to the minimum. Another reason for the large weight increases was that the wing was redesigned to incorporate thermal de-icing.

It was suggested that installation of Rolls-Royce Griffon engines would benefit the Windsor in view of the weight increase and would permit an increase to 73,670lb. With Griffons and at existing weights the maximum speed would be 390mph, and cruising speed restored to 321mph, at 23,000ft, but considerable redesign of the structure would have been necessary, with a hold-up in time scale, and this was not acceptable.

By the autumn of 1943 the first Windsor prototype, DW506, was completed and on 23 October Captain 'Mutt' Summers took the new bomber into the air for the first time, flying from Farnborough, Hants. This flight was made at a take-off weight of 46,000lb and during its early flights DW506 reached a speed of 302mph at 25,000ft.

Satisfactory flight characteristics were recorded at up to 54,000lb, but some wrinkling of the fabric covering was noticed as test flying progressed. After a number of flights at the low weight of 46,000lb the weak mixture cruising speed was established at 300mph at 23,000ft. During these flights the aircraft carried ballast in place of armament and bombs and very little Service equipment was installed, so the prototype was not representative of the production-type.

By now, three hundred Windsor B.Mk1s were on order, but the programme received a set-back when, after 33hr 45min flying time, DW506 ran into trouble during a test flight being carried out by a Service pilot from Boscombe Down. The circumstances of the accident are obscure, but the pilot seems to have had some difficulty with a propeller and made an emergency landing at Grove airfield, near Wantage, Berks. In the resulting crash DW506 broke its back and was damaged beyond repair.

Following this accident there were controversial exchanges between Boscombe Down and certain departments of the Air Ministry. There was some criticism of the pilot, albeit before the enquiry had been carried out, but the single-pilot layout caused considerable controversy. As access to the pilot's compartment was difficult it was almost impossible for any other crew member to assist the pilot in such an emergency by taking certain necessary actions, in particular in relation to engine controls and instruments. While there were many single-pilot aeroplanes flying, most of these in the larger category were twin-engined types, but the Windsor was bigger than a Lancaster and much more complicated than any twin-engined bomber. Another undesirable feature of the existing layout was that if the pilot was severely injured in action it was almost impossible to remove him from the cockpit or for any other crew member with flying experience to take over, in the way that was possible in Lancasters and Halifaxes. Added to this was the possibility of pilot fatigue after many hours over enemy territory.

It is surprising that the similar drawback of the Handley Page Hampden was not considered by Vickers or the Air Staff when the pilot's compartment was designed. Handley Page had adopted the single-pilot layout to lessen fuselage drag, with some justification

because the Hampden was a comparatively small twin-engined bomber, but some of the problems previously mentioned had been encountered on operations, notably pilot fatigue on even medium range flights. The Windsor was expected to make operational flights of ten or more hours' duration.

The second prototype, DW512, made it first flight, this time from the Vickers airfield at Wisley, on 15 February 1944, in the hands of Maurice Summers. It differed from the first aircraft in being powered by Merlin 85 engines in the then-new circular cowlings with annular radiators. Other changes included an extension to the top of the fin and rudder, equipment changes and the installation of a considerable amount of armour plate, all of which contributed to a big increase in the all-up weight. Despite this, the higher power of the Merlin 85s bestowed the second Windsor with similar characteristics to the ill-fated first prototype. Weak mixture cruising speed was 305mph at 23,000ft.

The test flying of DW512 brought a new problem, which was beginning to be evident on the first aircraft just before its accident: the fabric covering tended to stretch and deform as flying time increased, causing ballooning of the covering. As it got worse so did the flying characteristics worsen, notably at the stall, and eventually a large piece of fabric was torn away from the aircraft during a test flight. DW512 had to be grounded while the wings were re-covered with a glasscloth-backed fabric, but a new heavyweight wire mesh-backed fabric was developed for the third prototype.

Early in 1944 the estimated all-up weight of the production Windsor B.1 had risen to 76,000lb, a big increase in an aeroplane that was originally estimated to weigh 55,000lb, and on 14 March 1944, it was proposed that two Merlin versions should be produced, the standard fully armed and equipped Mk I and a lightened version with reduced equipment and without the barbettes (although what defensive armament was to be carried is obscure). The lightened version was estimated to carry 4,000lb of bombs for 4,000 miles.

As the weight of the Windsor rose the installation of Griffon engines was again considered, with the all-up weight at 88,341lb. This version looked attractive, restoring the performance lost by the continual weight increases, and it was the intention of the Air Ministry to order two Griffon-powered prototypes. Other engine installations were considered, including Bristol Centaurus and Hercules sleeve-valve radial engines. Estimates made in April 1944 showed that the Hercules-powered Windsor would have a top speed of 374mph and weak mixture cruise would be 312mph. At

Below left: The first prototype Vickers Windsor, DW506, at the Royal Aircraft Establishment, Farnborough, Hants, in October 1943. Note the sagging outer wings.

Above right: The first prototype Windsor on test.

Below: The second Windsor prototype, DW512, seen here, was heavier than its predecessor because of armour plating and other modifications.

weak mixture cruise 10,000lb of bombs could be carried for 1,770 miles, 6,000lb of bombs for 2,320 miles and 2,000lb of bombs for 2,800 miles. At the most economical cruising speed, 10,500lb of bombs could be carried for 2,220 miles, 6,500lb of bombs for 2,915 miles and 2,500lb for 3,620 miles.

The third prototype Windsor, NK136, was much more representative of a production B.Mk 1. It was powered by four Merlin 85 engines in circular nacelles, was equipped with the 20mm gun barbettes for the first time and carried operational equipment. NK136 proved to be considerably slower than the original estimates and at a loaded weight of 60,000lb the weak mixture cruising speed was only 280mph, while at 65,000lb the speed dropped to 264mph. Why this prototype should have been so much slower than the earlier Windsors remains a mystery but possibly the drag of the huge, blunt barbettes at the end of the outer nacelles was considerably higher than estimated. Apart from its slower speed this prototype continued to perform satisfactorily for about a year and its tests included air-firing the 20mm guns over Lyme Bay, Dorset. A similar prototype, NK138, was ordered, but not built. By now the provision for two .303in fixed guns in the nose had been deleted to provide space for the *H2S* scanner.

Disquiet over the single-pilot cockpit and defensive armament led to discussion of a redesign of the Windsor fuselage for production aircraft. As the bomber was likely to have a lower performance than was hoped for, and to make it capable of surviving on daylight operations, it was proposed that the barbette armament should be replaced by conventional turrets. The RAE had devised a universal bomber nose, with two .5in guns and a special 'bay window' for the bomb aimer, consisting of multiple optically-flat transparent panels, and this, after test flights on a Lancaster, had been adopted for the Avro Lincoln. A revised fuselage was projected for the Windsor using the RAE nose and front turret, a mid-upper Martin A3 turret housing two .5in guns and a twin .5in ball turret in the ventral position protecting the blind spot under the tail. It was suggested that the *H2S* radar scanner could be housed in a large fairing mounted on a pylon under the nose. Provision was made for a new cockpit layout with two pilots seated side by side.

While these developments were being drafted preparations for

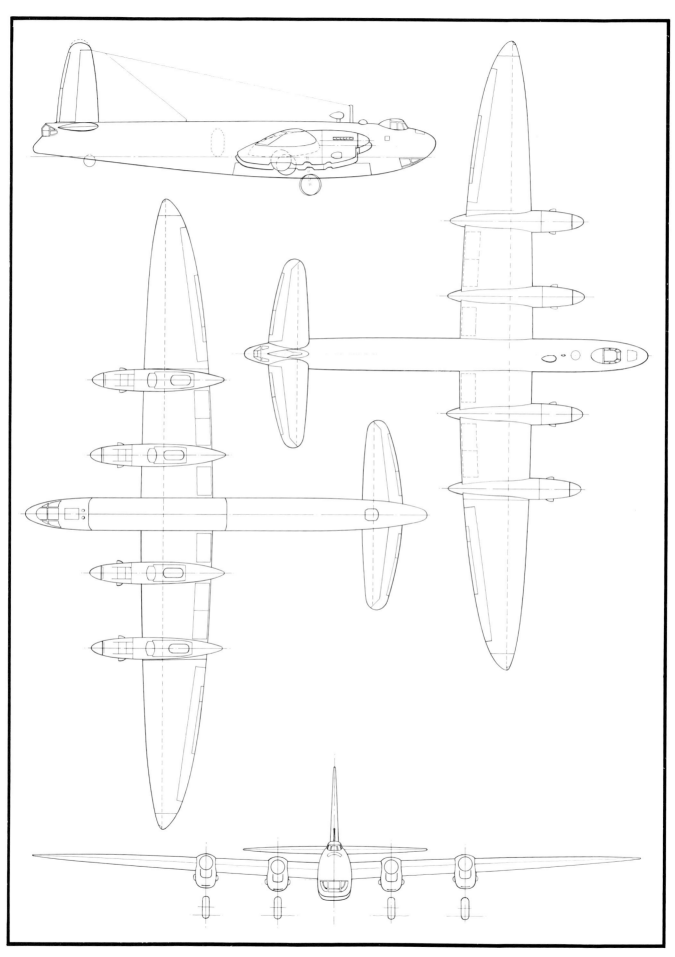

Far left: Vickers Windsor prototypes DW506 and DW512.

Left: Converted as a flying test bed for the original B.3/42 design's barbette armament was the second prototype Warwick, L9704, which was subsequently used for development of the Windsor's barbette armament. The only Windsor to actually fly with the barbette installations was the third prototype, NK136.

Below left: A barbette with two 0.5in guns mounted side-by-side in the second prototype Warwick, L9704.

Below: View of the barbette which was installed in the third prototype Windsor, NK136. Note that the twin 20mm cannon are mounted one above the other.

Bottom: Vickers Windsor with four Rolls-Royce Clyde turboprop engines.

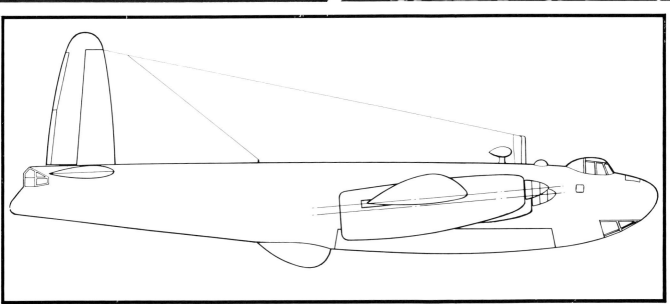

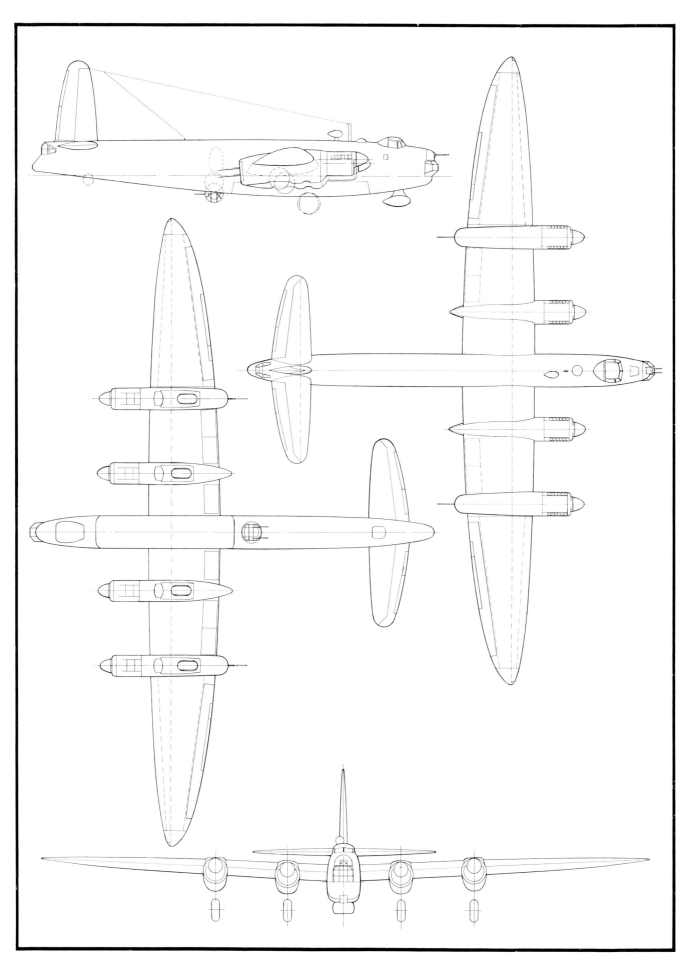

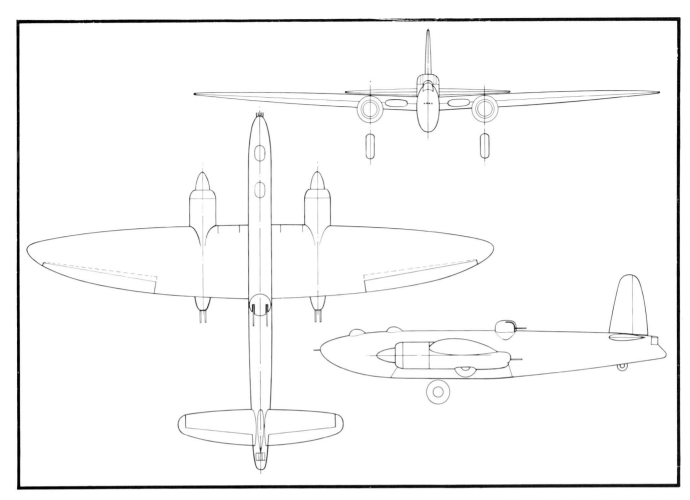

Left: One of the proposals for the production-type Windsor incorporating the RAE front gun and bomb aimer's position and Sperry ball turret. H2S radar would have been carried in the special fairing under the nose.

Above: Vickers B.3/42 powered by two Centaurus engines. The Vickers Warwick with gun barbettes in the end of each nacelle was a test vehicle for this project.

production of the Windsor were being made, but it seemed probable that the main production type would be much revised from the existing prototypes. Orders for the Merlin-powered Windsor B.Mk 1 had been progressively reduced. At first 300 were on order, but this had been reduced to 100, and subsequently to 40 aircraft. As later versions of the Windsor were projected with alternative engines, these began to look much more promising and the order for Mk Is was reduced to a few aircraft.

Towards the later stages of the war in Europe, Britain was developing a formidable array of turbine-engine designs, not only in the pure jet field but also in propeller-turbine engines. In 1943 Rolls-Royce began design work on an advanced propeller-turbine engine called the RB39, later given the name Clyde. The Clyde gave an initial power output of 3,000 shaft horsepower at a much lower weight than equivalent piston engines, and with considerably improved fuel consumption over pure jet engines. Progress with the Clyde was such that the first engine was ready for bench testing in December 1944. The new engine was almost twice as powerful as the Merlin, and Vickers naturally considered it as being very suitable for installation in the Windsor. The Clyde-engined Windsor, designated the Type 601 Windsor B.II, was expected to weigh 90,800lb fully-loaded. At 25,000ft, carrying 8,000lb of bombs, it was expected to fly for 2,910 miles at 396mph or 2,570 miles at 419mph. With the same load and at 35,000ft it could fly for 3,580 miles at 368mph and 3,160 miles at 388mph. With a

13,000lb bomb load at 25,000ft the Windsor B.II could fly for 2,530 miles at 396mph and 3,120 miles at 368mph.

So impressive were these performance figures that defensive armament was considered unnecessary, the bomber relying, like the Mosquito, on speed to evade fighters. The fuselage would be redesigned to have side-by-side seating for the pilots, turrets removed and possibly a dorsal fin to increase directional stability. A pressure cabin to enable the bomber to operate at the most efficient height for the turbine engines was another possible development. A prototype powered by four Clydes, NN670, was ordered and on 19 June 1945 it was decided that the main production Windsors would be of the Mk II version, preceded by a few Merlin-powered aircraft. Full production would commence in July 1946.

Unfortunately the plans for the Clyde-Windsor were not realised: only eleven Clyde engines were eventually built before the development of the engine was abandoned in favour of Nene, Derwent, Avon and Dart production. By 1946 the RAF had become committed to plans for all future combat aircraft, bombers and fighters to be pure-jet-powered, and the propeller-turbine engine did not fit into this future pattern. (Other propeller-turbine-engined aircraft, like the Athena and Balliol trainers, suffered the indignity of being re-engined with Merlin piston engines because of these future plans). Full production of the aircraft did not commence as planned and on 12 November 1945 the whole Windsor project was cancelled. With the Avro Lincoln entering service, and having a similar performance to the Merlin-powered Windsor, there was little justification in producing the B.I in large numbers, but the Clyde-Windsor could have provided a useful stage in the transition from the piston-engined heavy bombers to the V-bombers.

The Avro Lincoln

Second prototype Lincoln on test with full armament installed. Twenty squadrons flew Lincolns postwar and the type was a useful stop-gap pending the arrival of the first jet bomber in the shape of the English Electric Canberra.

To meet a requirement for a long-range heavy bomber for use in the Far East, outlined in Specification B.14/43, Avro produced a stretched version of the Lancaster, known as the Type 694. It retained the general geometry of the Lancaster, but the wing span was increased to 120ft and the fuselage length to 78ft 3½in.

The first drawings were issued in September 1943 and the prototype of what was then known as the Lancaster IV, PW925, first flew at Ringway, near Manchester, on 9 June 1944, piloted by Capt H. A. Brown. Handling was good although it was afterwards deemed necessary to fit larger trim tabs to the rudders. A second prototype, PW929, flew on 9 November 1944, and this machine, together with the third prototype, PW932, flown a year later (and long after the first production models), differed from PW925 in having a Bristol Type 17 dorsal turret housing two 20mm Hispano cannon instead of the former Martin turret housing two .5in machine guns. All subsequent production aircraft had the Bristol

turret. The Boulton Paul F-type nose turret was remotely controlled from the bomb aimer's position in the RAE-designed 'greenhouse' below and sighted by a periscopic Mk IIIM gunsight. The nose and rear turrets both had twin .5in Browning guns, the Boulton Paul D-type rear turret being controlled by a radar scanner in the extreme tail of the aircraft. The original design embodied a ventral gun position but as the *H2S* radar scanner was a more essential item, the idea was dropped.

Four 1,750hp Rolls-Royce Merlin 85s powered the Lancaster B.Mk IV, while the B.Mk V had their American-built equivalents, Packard Merlin 68As. The engines were housed in armour-plated annular-type cowlings similar in appearance to the cowlings of the Lancaster B.VI. So extensively did the basic design differ from the standard Lancaster that the Lancasters B.IV and B.V were soon renamed Lincoln B.I and B.II respectively, having the Avro Type number 694.

Production of the Lincoln was delayed by problems in switching over from Lancasters and although almost 100 Lincolns, mostly Mk Is, had been delivered to the RAF by VJ-Day, they did not see war service due to engine teething troubles and other technical problems. Lincoln production in Britain was handled by Avro (at Manchester and Yeadon), Metrovick and Armstrong Whitworth, but the large wartime orders were drastically reduced when peace came and the total number eventually built was 528, the Lincoln becoming the early postwar backbone of Bomber Command. Canada and Australia also decided to build Lincolns during the war. In Canada's case the decision was taken soon after VE-Day, and although no time was lost in starting production at Victory

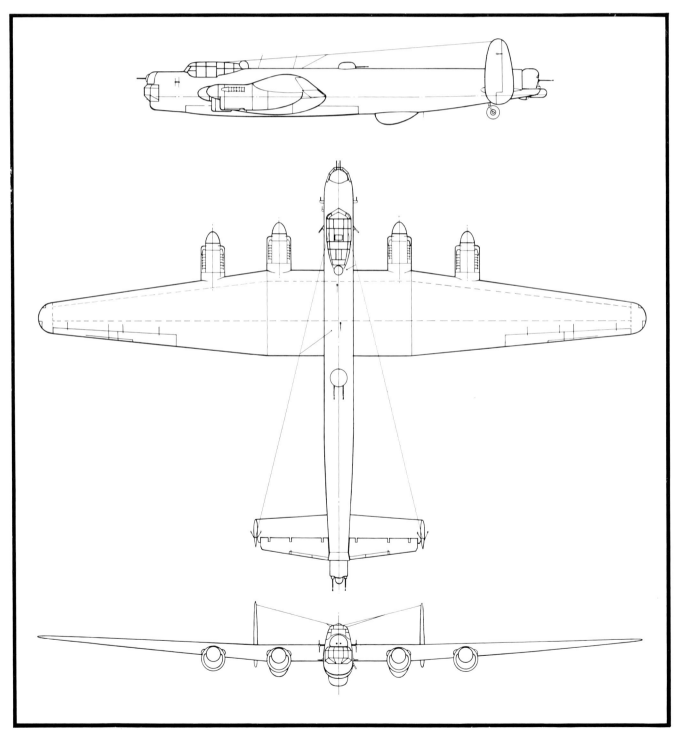

Left: Avro Lincoln. Originally known as the Lancaster Mk IV, the Lincoln was essentially a 'stretched' Lancaster with a new wing and engine nacelles.

Above: The Lincoln first flew in June 1944 and although deliveries were made to the RAF before World War II ended it did not begin to reach the squadrons in numbers until 1946. Shown is the first prototype, without armament.

Below: Close up of the nose of an early Lincoln of No 57 Squadron, first squadron to use the bomber, showing to advantage the Royal Aircraft Establishment-designed 'glasshouse' for the bomb aimer.

Aircraft of Canada, which also built the Lancaster B.X, only one Lincoln, B.XV FM300, had been completed by VJ-Day; Canadian production then ceased. Australia began preparations to build Lincolns in 1944 but production aircraft from Australian Government Aircraft Factory at Fisherman's Bend did not appear until after the war, the Lincoln being adopted by the RAAF who used it in several marks for many years.

The Lincoln B.I weighed 36,900lb empty, 68,000lb loaded (70,000lb with 22,000lb bomb), had a maximum speed of 287mph at 11,500ft and cruised at 210mph. Range was 1,660 miles with 14,000lb of bombs, 1,040 miles with a 22,000lb bomb and dorsal turret deleted. Service ceiling was 24,500ft.

Giant Bombers

By 1942 the future pattern of the bomber offensive against Germany had been established, with the USAAF heavy bombers carrying out massed formation attacks by day and the RAF continuing the offensive at night with massive saturation attacks against area targets. For this reason it seemed desirable to develop a series of heavy bombers for future production much larger than the Halifax and Lancaster, some three or four times larger in terms of all-up weight, and capable of carrying large numbers of heavy bombs or operating over very long ranges with a substantial bomb load. The Air Ministry invited companies to submit their proposals for very large bombers and Avro, Handley Page, Bristol, Shorts and Vickers put forward fifteen project designs between them.

Avro submitted two types, one with eight 2,000hp class engines and a loaded weight of 176,000lb and the other with ten 2,000hp class engines and a weight of 220,000lb. The smaller design had a wing loading of 60lb/sq ft and a bomb load of 19,500lb, could be carried over long ranges. The larger aircraft had the lower wing

loading of 45lb/sq ft and carried 15,000lb of bombs over a very long range. In each case the engines were mounted in separate nacelles driving tractor counter-rotating propellers.

Three of the projects put forward were designed by Handley Page, but two of the layouts were unconventional. The conventional type was to be powered by four 3,000hp Napier Sabre engines driving pusher propellers, the engines being housed in separate nacelles. This bomber carried a payload (fuel and bombs in varying proportions) of 60,000lb, and the estimated cruise speed was 332mph. The all-up weight was 157,000lb and wing loading 60lb/sq ft. The second project had the same all-up weight, engine installation and aspect ratio, but was of tail-first layout and smaller. It could carry a payload of 69,000lb and cruise at 354mph. The third design was the only jet-powered entry, and again of tail-first layout. It was powered by eight jet engines, and carried a maximum bomb load of 48,000lb, and cruised at 500mph at 40,000ft. Like the previous design its wing loading was above 72lb/sq ft. To lessen the take-off run power-assistance was used. This aircraft also weighed 157,000lb.

Bristols designed two projects, one with a loaded weight of 170,000lb, and powered by eight Rolls-Royce Griffon engines in coupled pairs driving contra-props, and the other weighing 220,000lb and powered by eight Bristol Centaurus radial engines in

Below: Bristol design for a 100ton super bomber powered by eight buried Centaurus engines driving four propeller shafts. The aircraft was of similar size to the Convair B-36.

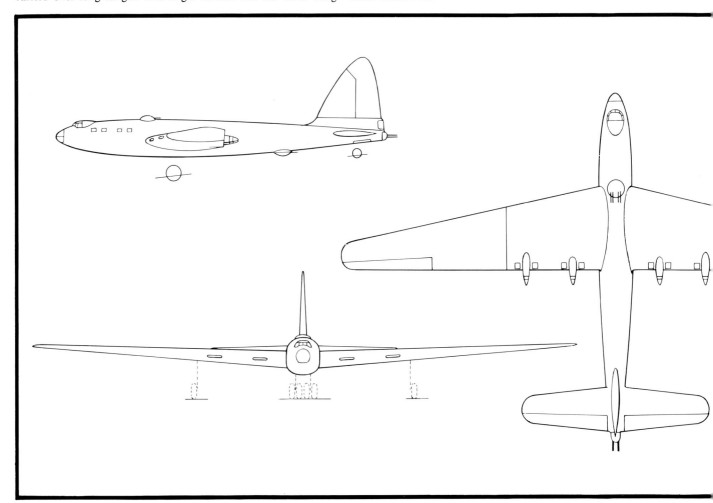

coupled pairs and, like the previous project, driving contra-props in pusher layout. (This latter design gave valuable design data for the Brabazon 1 eight-engined transport). Both aircraft used totally buried engines and vee-layout tails, without a vertical fin and rudder. The larger of the two had a wing span of 220ft and carried a maximum bomb load of 39,000lb, at an estimated cruising speed of 315mph at 25,000ft. Maximum fuel load was 6,800 gallons.

Shorts Bros' big bomber design was six-engined and conventional in layout, with all-up weights around 170-180,000lb. The bomber had a wing span of 168ft and versions were projected powered by Bristol Centaurus, Bristol Orion and Napier Sabre engines. A 25,500lb bomb load was to be carried at a cruising speed between 302 and 329mph at 25,000ft.

Vickers submitted five projects, all powered by six Bristol Centaurus engines and, as usual, all were geodetic in construction. Two of the designs were based on conventional layouts and weighed 168,000lb each. One of these two projects had pusher propellers, the other tractor layout and both carried a maximum bomb load of 65,000lb. The cruising speed was 317mph at 20,000ft. These two conventional projects featured unusual undercarriage arrangements, one having six single mainwheel units, one to each nacelle, whereas the second had four undercarriage units with six mainwheels on each unit, 24 wheels on the main undercarriage to spread the great weight out along the span.

Two other projects were tail-first designs, with fore-planes. One of these had six separate nacelles, with six Centaurus engines, while the other had two coupled Centaurus engines in each inner nacelle and a single Centaurus in each outer nacelle. The project with six separate nacelles had a main undercarriage housing a single wheel in each nacelle, but the second tail-first design featured four main undercarriage units with six wheels on each. Both projects had estimated weights of 178,000lb and cruised at 317mph. They carried a bomb/fuel load of 55,000lb.

One big advantage with the tail-first designs was that the rear defence, with heavy guns situated at the end of the fuselage and in the end of the nacelles, had uninterrupted fields of fire. The special RAE bomber nose, as used on the Lincoln, was designed into these projects.

The fifth Vickers project had a loaded weight of 174,000lb and was a tailless design, powered by six Centaurus engines buried in the wing and driving pusher propellers. This aircraft had an estimated cruise speed of 330mph at 20,000ft, and carried a payload (bombs and fuel in various combinations) of 65,000lb. The wing had a sweep-back of 15degrees, an aspect ratio of 7.4 and a loading of 43.5lb/sq ft.

Although probably designed to meet a different set of requirements from those laid down for the very large bombers mentioned, Miles submitted to the Air Ministry designs for a six-Centaurus-powered tail-first heavy bomber, based on experience gained with their B.11/14 project. This aircraft had an all-up weight of 150,000lb and could carry a maximum bomb load of 51,000lb.

Development and production of one or more of these super heavy bombers, which would have been comparable to the Convair B-36, would have been desirable from the point of view of providing even greater striking power from Bomber Command, but the production capacity of the British Aircraft Industry was already stretched to the limit and the disruption that would have resulted from changing over to new types of heavy bomber could only have lessened the production and striking power of existing types. The war, too, was reaching a turning point and none of these types could have been brought into service before 1945-46 at the earliest. The decision was therefore taken not to proceed further with these designs, but instead to concentrate on the Halifax, Lancaster, Lincoln and Windsor. The designs did, however, provide useful data for postwar civil aircraft, in particular the Bristol Brabazon 1, which used many of the design features of the big Bristol bombers.

Jet Bomber Projects

Gloster's chief designer, George Carter, while continuing development of jet-propelled fighters, also turned his attention to the problem of adapting the new form of power to produce a high-speed bomber. Even though the F.9/40 (Meteor) prototypes were still at the drawing board stage in development, Carter was already drafting ideas for jet-bombers.

Jet-propulsion units during the early 1940s were comparatively low-powered, in the 1,500-2,600lb thrust class, and therefore any project for a jet-bomber had to be multi-engined and of modest size. Carter's first detailed project was for a medium bomber with four Whittle engines having a span of 84ft and a length of 62ft 6in. Two versions of this design were drafted, one with four separate nacelles faired into the wings and slightly underslung, and the second with two engines in a single, centrally mounted nacelle on each wing. The nacelle design on the second project was in the form of horizontal elliptical sections, with horizontal elliptical intake for the two engines.

The fuselage design on both types featured a smooth, glazed nose housing the crew, and the tail unit was similar to that used on the Meteor. The aircraft had an internal bomb bay, with conventional doors, and, like the Meteor, was equipped with a tricycle undercarriage.

With four Whittle W.2B engines of some 2,000lb thrust each these initial projects were expected to have a maximum speed of 454mph at 36,000ft. The design was intended to cruise at well over 400mph and operate normally at between 40-45,000ft. Maximum normal bomb load was to be 4,000lb, with twice that weight of bombs in the overload condition, similar to the much slower, armed, piston-engined day bombers then under development. Maximum range was intended to be 1,500 miles, with an additional 20min reserve over the target.

Considering the early stage of development of jet-propulsion power units at the time this project may have been rather ambitious, but the similar Arado 234, which was only two-thirds the size of the Gloster project, showed that such a bomber was quite a feasible proposition. In its twin-engined form the Arado, with a span of 46ft 3½in, had a similar performance, but had much less range and only half the maximum bomb load. Carter's bomber was also intended to fly some 20,000ft higher than the Arado at both cruising and maximum ceiling.

Further development of his bomber projects resulted in a four-engined jet aircraft (again with two engines in one nacelle on each wing) with a wing span of 100ft and an overall length of 72ft. Fuselage diameter was 7ft. Maximum all-up weight was 36,000lb, and the following bomb loads were specified: 6 x 1,000lb; 9 x 500lb; 9 x 250lb; 4 x 1,000lb and 3 x 500lb; or 1 x 4,000lb HC. The leg to the target was to be flown at 395mph at 40,000ft, increasing to 405mph over the target, and after climbing to 45,000ft the normal cruising speed would be around 400mph. Overload range was expected to be 1,500 miles. For operations at these heights the aircraft was, of course, to be fully pressurised.

Whereas the Arado 234 entered service, Carter's projects remained purely examples of what might be achieved with the power available. Specifications were not drawn up for them, but they did provide a basis for discussion into future medium bomber requirements which were ultimately to lead to the Canberra twin-engined bomber of similar size and operating height.

The Air Staff's requirement for a new night/medium bomber was incorporated in Specification B.3/45, and the new bomber was to be jet-powered. Although most of the project development of the B.3/45 design commenced after the end of the war, the resultant twin-jet bomber, the English Electric Canberra, originated at Westland Aircraft where Mr W. E. W. Petter, who was responsible for the Canberra design, was Technical Director before taking up the similar appointment with English Electric. In 1943-44 Petter commenced draft studies for a high-speed twin-engined jet-propelled fighter-bomber. During the course of development two separate projects were evolved, both powered by two Metropolitan-Vickers F.2/Mk IV axial-flow turbines — which were the most advanced in design of all the British turbine designs of that period (there was actually a ducted fan variant of this basic design under development — some 10-15 years earlier than the now-accepted fan engines for airliner power). Of somewhat similar configuration, these two projects, the P.1056 and P.1061, differed fundamentally in undercarriage design, the P.1056 having the then-orthodox tail-down type and the P.1061 having a tricycle undercarriage. The P.1061 featured a large internal bomb bay, and both types had four fixed 20mm cannon in the lower part of the front fuselage. The two F.2 turbines were mounted side-by-side in the upper part of the centre fuselage, with air being fed from a large nose intake of horizontal elliptical form. Whereas the P.1056 had two separate jet pipes, the P.1061 had the two pipes merging into a single jet exhaust. In both projects the two crew members were housed in the extreme nose, protected by a single 'bubble' canopy — the seats being side-by-side.

After Petter moved to English Electric he continued work on the bomber design, but this time the aircraft was redesigned around the power of a single, large turbine engine fed with air from intakes in the wing leading edges. The fixed armament was dispensed with, and the new arrangement of engine and intakes permitted the upper part of the centre fuselage to be entirely taken up by a fuel tank, while the lower part formed the bomb bay capable of carrying six 1,000lb bombs. A crew of three was housed in the pressurised nose and protected by a 'bubble' canopy.

After this the design moved away from the earlier configuration and gradually evolved into the English Electric B.3/45 twin-Rolls-Royce Avon-powered bomber, ordered under the type name Canberra — but this was a postwar development and is thus outside the scope of this book.

Other jet-bomber projects of the war years, none of which was built, were the development of the Miles B.11/41 twin-Merlin tandem-wing medium bomber powered by three Whittle-type jet engines and studies by Handley Page and Gloster for very large heavy bombers powered by multiple Whittle engines, eight in the case of Handley Page's 500mph design. Gloster's design was of all-wing layout, with Whittle engines buried inside the wings and fed from leading edge intakes.

Above right: To test their B.11/41 project design, Miles Aircraft built and flew this ⅝ scale flying model powered by two DH Gypsy Major engines and designated Miles M39B.

Below right: Mr W. G. Carter's Gloster jet bomber design powered by four Whittle-type jet engines.

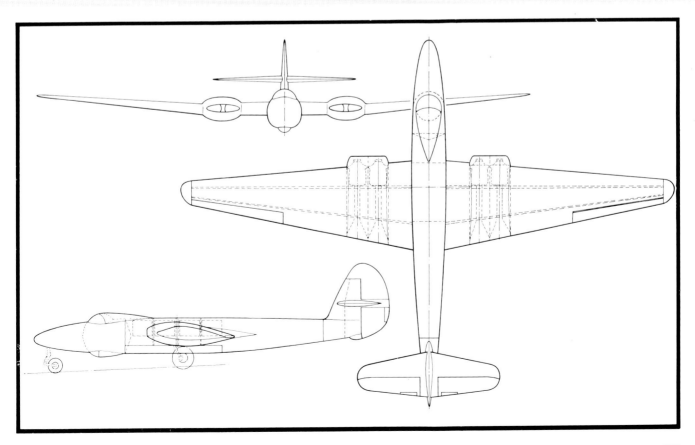

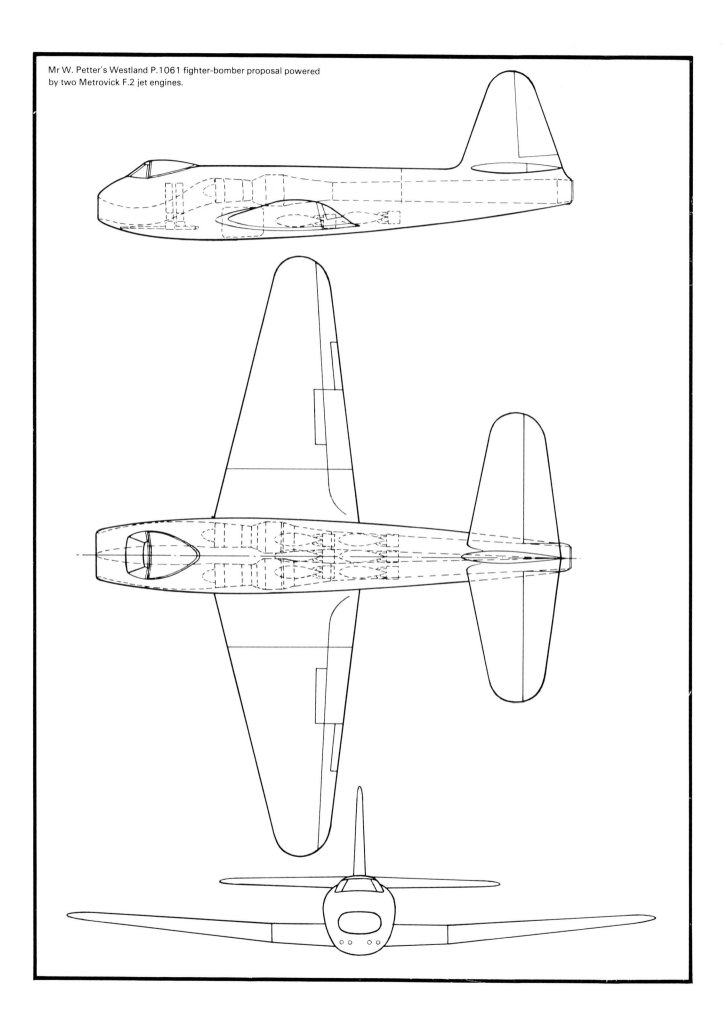

Mr W. Petter's Westland P.1061 fighter-bomber proposal powered
by two Metrovick F.2 jet engines.